CW01311035

CHI GONG
Medicine From
GOD

3rd EDITION

Myung Chill Kim

CHI GONG: Medicine From GOD
By Myung Chill Kim

Published by Seven Galaxy Publications™
Copyright © 1999
First Revision (2nd Edition) 2006
Second Revision (3rd Edition) 2022
by Myung Chill Kim

All rights reserved. No part of this book may be reproduced without the author's written permission.

www.kwangmooryu.com

CHI GONG: Medicine from GOD/ by Myung Chill Kim
3rd Edition

Library of Congress Control Number: 2021925488

$19.95

About the Author

Myung Chill Kim was born in Korea in 1942. He is the seventh child in a family of eleven brothers and sisters and has lived with Oriental Martial Arts and Oriental Medicine for his entire life. He is the 37th generation Doctor of Oriental Medicine in his family.

He moved to the United States in 1970. His first book, "Acupuncture for Self-Defense," was published in 1971. This book deals with acupuncture or pressure points to paralyze or heal an opponent.

His second book, "Oriental Medicine and Cancer," was published in 1998. This book deals with the general theory of Oriental Medicine. It emphasizes Chi (Qi) energy theory and his new discovery of the causative factors of cancer in modern times, such as sports injuries, car accident injuries and surgical scars, which block the Chi flow in acupuncture channels.

He performed acupuncture anesthesia in June of 1973 at the Naval Hospital at Portsmouth, Virginia.

Myung Chill Kim attended New York City Technical College for three years to study Western science. He graduated from the Emperor's College of Oriental Medicine in 1984 and received his degree of Doctor of Oriental Medicine in 1988, from Samra University of Oriental Medicine.

He discovered the main causative factor of cancer by applying his martial-art-and-acupuncture-channel theory, developed through his clinical research of acupuncture and herbal medicine in the United States, during the last 50 years.
Currently, Myung Chill Kim practices acupuncture and herbal medicine in Oklahoma City, Oklahoma.

Dedication

This book is dedicated to the memory of my grandmother, who used to tell me many interesting stories. In 1948, my family last visited my grandmother in the beautiful countryside. We were preparing to escape to South Korea from the communist North. We could not tell my grandmother but needed to keep this a secret. I could sense that this would be the last time I saw my grandmother, but had to say, "I'll see you again, Grandma!" I was only six years old.

Acknowledgments

I would like to express my appreciation to the following friends: Sue Macy, Michael Kopel, and Thomas Arnold, without whose rigorous writing and typing efforts this book would never have come to be.

My thanks also go to Master Chen Yo Yu for his Chinese calligraphy. Most drawings were beautifully done by Lisa Allen and Ian Factor; other drawings and the cover design of the 2nd revised edition was done by Joseph Deluca.

My thanks also to Hunhee Lee for the book design of the 1st edition. Thanks to Sue Macy for editing the 1st edition and to Loren Miner for the final edit.

I would like to give thanks to Lisa Dixon, Greg Dixon, Raynee Bradley, Roger Blasius and for demonstrating poses in photos.

My thanks also to Hester Anne Brown for editing the 3rd edition, and to Raye Frerer for editing and page layout assistance. Also, many thanks to Steve Eagleston who proofread this book.

Finally, I would like to thank my wife Sungchu and my children John and Stella, and other family members for their continued support.

Warning – Disclaimer

This book is intended to provide information on the general theory of Chi Gong.

The theories of Oriental Medicine discussed in this book were adopted to allow for the differences between the Western and Eastern lifestyles. It is intended for use by laymen as well as other practitioners of alternative medicine. Western medical theory is not discussed here.

This book should only be used as a general guide and should not be considered the best, or only, source of information on medicine but rather as a new approach to medicine.

The author and Seven Galaxy Publications shall have neither liability nor responsibility to any person or organization with respect to any mental or physical damage caused directly or indirectly by the information in this book.

Chi Gong

Energy and Effort

Table of Contents

Introduction 15

Chapter 1 History of Chi Gong...............................17

Chapter 2 Yin/Yang Theory....................................21

Chapter 3 Learning and Practicing Chi Gong........23

    Martial Arts Chi Gong (Internal Style).......23

    Zen Meditation...25
    Taoist Chi Gong...31
    Buddhist Chi Gong 49
    Chi Gong with Talisman Symbols............57
    Herbal Chi Gong 58
    Chanting 60
    Fasting...63
    Praying 73
    Chi Gong and Zen Differences.................74
    Speed of Chi 75
    Losing Weight through Breathing.............76
    "Bellow" Breathing....................................78
    Korean Martial Art Chi Gong....................80
    Korean Heat Chi Gong.............................81
    Delivering a Baby Easily...........................87
    Lie down and Stretch................................96
    Bottle...97
    Benefits of Crawling...............................100
    Building Sexual Energy..........................106
    How to Prevent Altitude Sickness..........112
    Divers' Sickness.....................................115
    Moxa (Self-Treatment) 116

Chapter 4	Experiences During Chi Gong......136
Chapter 5	Taoists I Have Met 141
Chapter 6	Acupuncture Channels................145
Chapter 7	Cautions with Chi Gong Practice...177
Chapter 8	The Future of Chi Gong...............191
Chapter 9	Questions and Answers..............193
	Taking Shoes Off at Home..........198
Chapter 10	Preventing and Treating COVID....201

Epilogue 206

Glossary 210

Index..212

INTRODUCTION

"Master Kim, we have so much Chi[1] energy, what should we do with it?" Sue and Judith asked me. They were in their 40s and students in my Chi Gong[2] class.

"Send Chi energy to your friends or relatives who live far from here, holding your palms together as in prayer," I replied.

"How far can it go?" they asked. "It can reach anywhere in the universe," I replied. They then inquired, "What will happen?" and I stated, "The receiver will think of you or dream of you, and then he/she will call you in the near future." The entire class then sent Chi to those far away.

The following week at the next class, Judith told the class that her brother in Florida, 1,500 miles away from Cambridge, Massachusetts, called her. This was the first time in 3 years. Sue said that her old boyfriend in Ireland called her, for the first time in over a year. The male students had no experiences to report, something that I expected.

Sometimes we talk about someone and if he or she appears, we say "Well, speak of the devil!" The Koreans say "Well, speak of the Tiger!" About 400 years ago, the Buddhist High Priest Suhsan[3] left Myohyung Mountain in the northwest part of Korea and traveled south for 200 miles to see his disciple, Sa Myung Dang[4]. As he approached the southern mountains, he met a young boy waiting for him at a creek. He asked the boy, "How did you know I would be here?" The boy replied, "The high priest Sa Myung Dang told me so."

Yogis in India and Taoist[5] Chi Gong masters can still to this day communicate with their colleagues by sending telepathic messages. Some mere mortals can as well, especially through dreams. For example, my friend's mother dreamed of her son's death the instant it occurred in the Vietnam war. His father did not. Chi Gong practice can help develop this ability and help us recognize and understand these experiences.

CHI
Energy

CHAPTER 1
History of Chi Gong

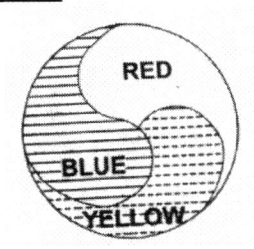

Fig. 1-1

A group of Korean Taoists greeted and welcomed with gestures, a Lama[6] from Tibet and a Taoist monk from China. They were in a dark cave lit only by a small torch on the cave wall. The Koreans smiled and showed sympathy for both of them.

While each spoke only his own language, it seemed as though they understood each other perfectly without any voice or sound, due to the highly developed perceptual skills developed though many years of Chi Gong meditation. The Tibetan and the Taoist had each traveled very long distances in very short times. The Tibetan traveled 9,000 miles across the Asian continent to the Korean peninsula by foot in 5 days. The Chinese monk traveled 1,000 miles to the same area from the Tai San[7] mountains in China in just one day. Both came through the mountains during the Cultural Revolution in China during the 1970s to avoid the border guards and others. Both were just ordinary human beings themselves. How were they capable of super-human feats like these? Why? Because they were Chi Gong masters who dwelled in mountain caves for 50 years or more.

You can have experiences similar to these. If you practice Chi Gong for one or two hours each day for 100 days, you will feel light on your feet when you walk, and you can go for a long distance without feeling tired.

It is difficult to historically define exactly what Chi Gong is. We can only guess at its origin, thousands of years ago in India and Tibet. It then spread through China to Korea. Chi Gong masters were called Yogi in India. Buddhist[8] priests called the practice Yoga or Zen meditation.

Taoists priests named the movement or meditation designed to increase and circulate vital energy Nei Gong (internal effort). This was further classified Tao Ren Breathing method, named for the Taoists who did not belong to a temple; otherwise known as the Tan Tien[9] Breath method. This practice was then christened Chi Gong in China during the 1960's. During the Cultural Revolution in China, the Taoists practiced only Chi Gong mediation, Tai Chi[10], fortune telling, or wrote talismans for the village people, rather than performing physical work. This type of "work" did not conform to the new Chinese philosophy, and the Communist youth burned most of the Taoist temples and killed or imprisoned the Taoists. The ones who escaped this fate hid in the mountains or in caves or ran away to other countries. There are still some old Taoist temples in China, including Ameipa for women.

Korea was much influenced by the Taoist and Tibetan traditions. Korean Taoism, especially in the costume and the manner is seen in the call to the dead, in the Chi Gong practices in both Shamanic cultures, and in the traditional drums used in ritual dancing, which are decorated with triple red, blue, and yellow fish-shaped symbols.

There are traces of Korean fasting in American culture. About 5,000 years ago, the mother of the first King of Korea was said to be a bear that fasted and prayed with a tiger for 100 days in a cave. She became a woman and bore her son, Dan Gun,[11] who became King.

Also, both Korean and Native Americans have the Mongolian spot – a blue spot like a bruise on the hip that babies are born with. This occurs in Eskimos and Native Americans. Both cultures decorate their hats with bird feathers and leave their dead bodies for the birds. Tibet has this burial custom too, know as Sky Burial.

Growing up in Korea, I heard many stories from my mother that as many as 100 Taoists would climb up to the mountains for a month of fasting and meditation, even during the busy farm seasons in the spring and fall. They were blamed for their selfishness by the villagers.

Sometimes they might imitate their leader or teacher who could jump or fly across cliff. Some would fall and die. Most developed extraordinary senses that would diminish a few months later. If a man's wife left his home and hid in that of another, he could locate her without looking. Or, if his wife served a fish to a guest who only ate part of it, then dressed it up and reserved it to her husband as though it were fresh, he could detect that it had been touched by others. Some became healers cured with their hands or acupuncture needles. Others could detect sickness by looking at the face of a patient. Still others could look into the body at the internal organs to make a diagnosis.

In the New Testament of the Bible, there are accounts of Jesus touching a dead child and bringing him back to life. A woman touched his robe and was healed of a chronic disease by the energy from his body. Shakyamuni Buddha[12] pointed his finger at a huge rock falling from a cliff directly above his head and it stopped. His voice stopped a herd of elephants, and his energy prevented a murderer from killing him. This murderer had the thumbs of 99 victims around his neck, and the Buddha was to be the 100th.

Experiences such as those above can be documented today. Once, in South Korea in 1995, a 5-story department store collapsed, killing many. Several days later, a professor was traveling to a college to give a lecture. He had a vision and went to the accident site. He told the workers to dig in a certain place. They ignored him. He persisted, and when they dug down 3 meters to where he instructed, they found a person still alive, and two bodies. This professor practiced meditation and Chi Gong every morning and his sixth sense and extra sensory perceptions were developed beyond the capacity of normal human beings.

CHAPTER 2
Yin/Yang Theory

Fig. 2-1

Fig. 2-2

Yin/Yang theory has its origins in the dualist philosophy of ancient India. In Sanskrit[13], the term Hatha, as in Hatha Yoga, has a similar meaning as Yin and Yang in Chinese. In India, it was thought that God and the Devil possessed similar abilities and co-existed in the world just as other dualities, like day and night, man and woman, Heaven and Earth.

I think of Yin/Yang not only as day and night but as sunset and dawn, the transitional moving stages between the opposite poles. We get Yang energy when we practice Chi Gong facing the sun, and Yin energy when we practice facing the moon. A few practice at midnight in the graveyard to receive energy from the dead, which is not recommended for my students.

借力

CHA RYUK

Borrowed Power

CHAPTER 3
Learning and Practicing Chi Gong

There are many styles of Chi Gong, but they fall within 10 major categories. I give lessons in most of the following Chi Gong styles, both through my classes in the New England area and through personalized information sent to out-of-state and foreign residents.

- Martial Arts Chi Gong (Internal Style) – Cha Ryuk Hap Ki Do
- Zen Meditation
- Taoist Chi Gong
- Buddhist Chi Gong
- Herbal Chi Gong
- Chi Gong with Talisman symbols
- Chanting Chi Gong
- Fasting (Diet) with seaweed
- Praying

Martial Arts Chi Gong (Internal Style)

With martial arts itself, there are two major styles – External and Internal. External style develops muscular strength, cardiovascular and pulmonary functions. Most of the Olympic sports, Karate[14], hard style Chinese Kung Fu[15], Tae Kwon Do[16], Judo[17], boxing, and wrestling are types of this form. Internal style is as the name implies; it is designed to build up chi energy through slow breathing exercises. Hap Ki Do[18] (Aikido[19] in Japanese), Xing Yi[20], Ba Gua[21], Tai Chi and Chi Gong fall within this grouping.

External　　　　　Internal
Movement becomes smaller and slower

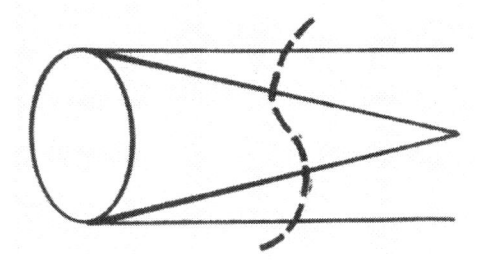

Fig. 3-1

External style – wears waist belt for muscular strength.
Internal style – wears loose clothing and no belt so as not to disturb Chi flow.

One needs to consider an opponent's physical and psychological make-up when practicing martial arts. But when practicing Chi Gong or Zen Meditation, you do not consider your opponent, but you should consider nature and the universe.

With external style practices, almost everyone's experiences of muscle soreness due to overexertion will be the same. But the build-up of Chi energy through internal practices affects each person differently. We will discuss this later in the Chapter.

I used to practice Cha Ryuk[22], more martial art than Chi Gong, when I first moved to the U.S. in the 1970's. The practice starts with Zen meditation, holding the breath for six minutes, then beating the stomach and chest area with one's fist to toughen the body and increase the Chi energy. I also did not spend much time practicing ordinary Chi Gong, as I was teaching Tae Kwon Do where I yelled, jumped, and breathed. Now, I focus my practice and teaching on the internal styles.

Hap Ki Do (Aikido in Japanese) is a self-defense art. Its technique is between Tae Kwon Do (Karate) and Judo (wrestling). It falls between internal and external martial arts. Some variations of Hap Ki Do emphasize the development of muscular strength and some styles focus on increasing Chi energy.

Zen Mediation is essential to an understanding of Oriental culture. The various styles come mainly from the Buddhist religion; others come from Taoist or Yoga tradition. Zen meditation is a form of mental practice which enables the practitioner to attain tranquility and peace of mind. It is not a form of prayer or worship, cannot be translated as meditation, and is not found in Western culture. Bodhidharma (circa 528 A.D.) first introduced Zen Buddhism to China. He was the 28th successor of Buddha, the third prince of the kingdom of Southern India and succeeded to the throne.

But he soon abdicated to his brother and traveled from India to China, where Buddhism was thriving. He visited the emperor of the Yang dynasty in Nanjing. Here he was not welcomed as he did not flatter the emperor, but rather tried to teach him the Zen meditation philosophy. He then crossed the Yangzi river to the Shaolin temple[23] where he taught martial arts, Chi Gong and Zen meditation. Later, he went into a cave for nine years and practiced Zen Meditation facing a wall. To this day, people still visit and pay their respects to Bodhidharma's statue in this cave.

Bodhidharma is not to be confused with Shakyamuni Buddha, the founder of Buddhism. Not only were they different people but their appearances were very different as well. Shakyamuni Buddha's head bulged at the top, due to the chi energy rising up to his head.

Bodhidharma's stomach was quite expansive, and the popular opinion was that this was due to his lack of exercise during the nine years of cave-dwelling. But this is not the case. He did not eat much and fasted most of the time during his prolonged period of Zen practice. His stomach bulged out because his chi energy was stored there.

Most beginners of Zen think that this practice is for emptying all thoughts, not to think at all:

> If worldly thoughts do occur, do not concentrate on banishing them, for you will only be thinking more thoughts instead of less. Simply continue your counting and try to concentrate on nothing other than your counting.

If you are obsessed by not thinking of anything, it is just like the power of a negative suggestion in self-hypnosis. It will only make you very uncomfortable.

What I recommend is my replacement theory. Whether or not you think of something, you can never rid yourself of Descartes law of "I think therefore I am." Therefore, you should concentrate on counting your breath or counting as many numbers as you can during a 10-minute period of time. If you do this, you will feel comfortable with breathing, find peace of mind and want to do this more and more – and you are already learning Zen. You may not feel the same as someone who has practiced for many years, but you will be experiencing Zen meditation.

There are many ways to practice Zen in yoga. One method is similar to self-hypnosis; another method is just to look at one object thoroughly and meditate on that object. For example, you can look at a flower and think about the process from seed to planting to growing.

Buddhist teachings describe many different mental stages you can achieve during Zen meditation throughout your lifetime. These stages were written in Sanskrit, Tibetan,

and Chinese languages. They cannot be translated accurately into the English language – the closest we can get to describing these stages in English are self-awareness, self-realization, enlightenment and nirvana. These stages cannot be measured or quantified but can only be felt or achieved naturally through many years of Zen practice.

It was communicated in a Korean newspaper during the 1950's that a Buddhist priest practiced Zen for 50 years but could not reach nirvana. He jumped into the lake and died sitting in the Zen mediation pose. This priest, like most people, could not reach nirvana during his lifetime like Shakyamuni Buddha did.

When a person dies, the Taoists describe it as the Chi leaving the body. Buddhist priests may say to the family of a dead one that they should rejoice, for at last, this person has reached nirvana.

A complicated series of martial arts movements, such as Tai Chi patterns, is called moving meditation. Three years ago, a woman visited me for a consultation. She had practiced Zen mediation for many years but she was unable to practice anymore – her 16 year-old son had died from cancer. I suggested that she learn Tai Chi. Six months later she returned, and said she felt better. So, I suggested that she begin practicing Zen meditation and Tai Chi together. A few weeks later she came back and told me that she could do both together easily. This is the perfect balance of Yin and Yang: non-moving Zen and moving Zen. Both of these will balance, harmonize and complement each other, both physically and mentally.

These days, children suffer from Attention Deficit Disorder (ADD). We should not suggest that they learn Zen meditation or Tai Chi. They need to and like to practice Tae Kwon Do, Karate, Shaolin Kung Fu, external-style martial arts, or western sports, such as soccer, football, tennis, and the like. These activities require more physical strength and produce more sweat. In fact, I often suggest to those 30 years of age or less that they first learn external-style martial arts forms, which have patterns of movements similar to Tai Chi but are more forceful and require more physical strength. Later, I advise those over 30 years of age to put in more time studying Zen.

How to practice Zen Mediation

- Sit on the floor in the lotus position (Figure 3-33). Your legs are crossed. If this position is difficult for you, sit in a chair.
- Look at one spot on the wall in front of you that is lower than eye-level or one that is three feet in front of you on the floor. Keep your eyes open, but if your eyes get tired, you can close them – but keep thinking about looking at the spot.
- Follow the following pattern. Note that there are many different ways to breath, and that you can invent your own pattern to suit your body condition or your needs. If you have weak organs or are sick, you will not be able to breathe longer than you usually do.

Inhale/Exhale through nose

Inhale count   Exhale count
   5...10

Stay with   5........10,   5..........10

If worldly thoughts occur, increase the count or reverse,
          6..........12,   7..........14,
          8..........16,   9..........18,
          10........20, and so on.

"I COUNT, THEREFORE I AM."
- Myung Kim

- Inhale and exhale one cycle of breathing, then fold on finger into your right hand, ten right-hand fingers equals one left-hand finger.
- When you exhale, you can count backwards too.

Side Effect of Zen Meditation

People attain tranquility and peace of mind thru Zen meditation. However, I also already mentioned the negative suggestion that if anyone understands that there are not many interferences to do Zen meditation. But after practicing Zen meditation, some people still felt irritability, anxiousness, sadness, and other emotionally negative side effects, etc. Usually one with severe stress, one with heart and /or kidney channel blocked syndrome, ones that are frightened easily, with many dreams, nightmares, lethargy and fearful feelings may experience these negative side effects. People with these symptoms should receive Acupuncture treatment, Herbal medicine, and Chi Gong training to strengthen the Heart and Kidney function before practicing Zen meditation.

Chi Gong (Qi Gong)

There are many styles of Chi Gong in China. You can see the people practice them in the parks each morning, and try a few yourself. There are also many styles of yoga in India, like Kundalini, which is similar to Chi Gong. I will focus on two main styles of Chi gong, Taoist and Buddhist.

Taoist style Chi Gong emphasizes the building up of sexual energy and technique, health and longevity though holding the breathing, contracting the anus muscle, and exhaling. Buddhist style is more spiritual in nature than chi energy cultivation. In Buddhist style, you inhale and exhale longer than your normal breathing pattern, like you are threading a fine thread through your nose, similar to Zen meditation.

Shakyamuni Buddha did not recommend "holding breathing method," as he thought it was too similar to death. Another way to look at it is that Taoists try to build up health and achieve longevity through Chi Gong practice, and Buddhists try to gain spirituality and Chi energy together.

Taoist Style Chi Gong

The following pages on Chi Gong (or Qi Gong) movements are extracted from the book *Oriental Medicine and Cancer*, by this author. If you feel the chi energy after you follow these instructions, then try the following Chi Gong exercise (Figures 3-2 through 3-20).

HOW TO DEVELOP CHI (INTERNAL ENERGY)

I have been teaching in the United States since my arrival in 1970. To learn meditation, Chi Gong, Tai Chi, martial arts or Oriental Medicine, students must be willing to devote the time and effort necessary to learn these arts. But the following three methods of breathing have been developed for easy learning so that people can gain some benefit and get a taste of Chi for themselves. Before practicing any of these exercises, rub your hands and feet for a few moments until they feel warm. Also keep in mind these guidelines.

General Guidelines for Chi Gong Practice

1. Face either East or South.

2. Practice at least one hour before or after eating.

3. Do not practice if you are overly tired, hungry, sick, or emotionally upset.

4. Chi Gong practice should leave one feeling calm and centered. Consult a Chi Gong master if you feel excessively joyful or sad after practicing.

5. Ideally, practice twice a day at sunrise and noon.

6. Do not practice at night before you go to sleep. It is best to have at least four hours between Chi Gong practice and going to bed.

7. Practice in a quiet, clean place and wear loose fitting clothes.

8. Breathe in and out through your nose deeply and slowly. Imagine your breath to be a fine continuous silken thread. Or breathe like a newborn baby taking a nap. Beginning students should do a short breathing cycle, inhaling for a count of five and exhaling for a count of ten. More advanced students will naturally do a longer cycle, perhaps inhaling for a count of ten and exhaling for a count of twenty, or even longer.

9. Never combine Chi Gong with weightlifting exercises or practice when you are intoxicated.

10. Pregnant women should avoid these exercises.

If you develop nausea, vomiting, a headache, or insomnia from Chi Gong practice, do the tension relief breathing exercises described below. Then immerse your hands and feet in warm water for ten minutes.

Kidney #1
Fig. 3-2

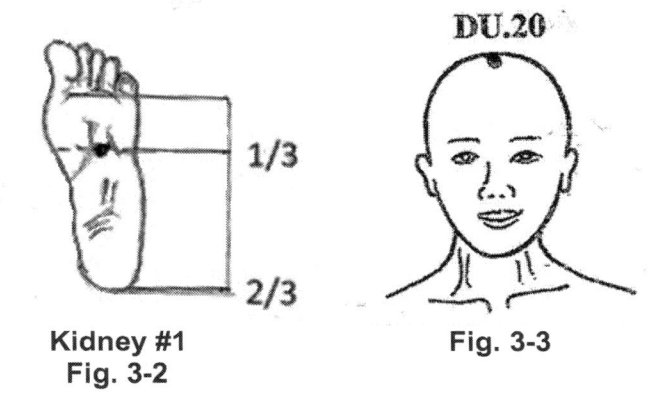

Fig. 3-3

Chi Gong breathing

1. Rub your hands and feet 30 times. Sit on a chair and hit Kid #1 point (Fig. 3-2) with the pinky side of your fist for 30 times. Rub the kidney area – just above the waistline, below both sides of the rib cages with your dorsal part of the wrist for 30 times. Hit the top of your head – GV. 20 point (Fig. 3-3) 30 times with the second knuckle of your fist.
2. Touch the tip of the tongue to the roof of the mouth.
3. Inhale through the nose, drawing your breath down into your lower abdomen. Hold your breath for a few seconds and then exhale very slowly through the nose. Exhalation should always be longer than inhalation.
4. It is possible that there may be an uncomfortable emotional and/or physical feeling, or insomnia after Chi Gong practice. In case of an emergency (nausea, vomiting, fainting, heart pain, dizziness or extreme tiredness), immerse both hands and feet in hot water for 10 minutes instead of rubbing them. You will then be able to gain back and regulate Chi energy much faster.

A. TENSION RELIEF BREATHING EXERCISES

1. Look straight ahead and focus your attention on a spot on the wall slightly below eye level.

2. Turn your hands so that the backs are facing forwards as shown in Figure 3-4.

3. Inhale deeply through your nose and draw your hands and forearms upward from your lower abdomen. Then rotate them outwards in a large circle. See Figures 3-4, 3-5, 3-6.

4. Push your palms forward with fingertips pointing towards the earth and exhale through your mouth, making the sound "ssshhh." Imagine that you are pushing out all your bad feelings, thoughts, and emotions along with your breath. See Figure 3-7.

5. If you feel angry, depressed, sad, or otherwise emotionally troubled, do these breathing exercises rapidly at first while gradually slowing down your rate of breathing. Repeat 10 to 20 times until you feel calmer.

Fig. 3-4

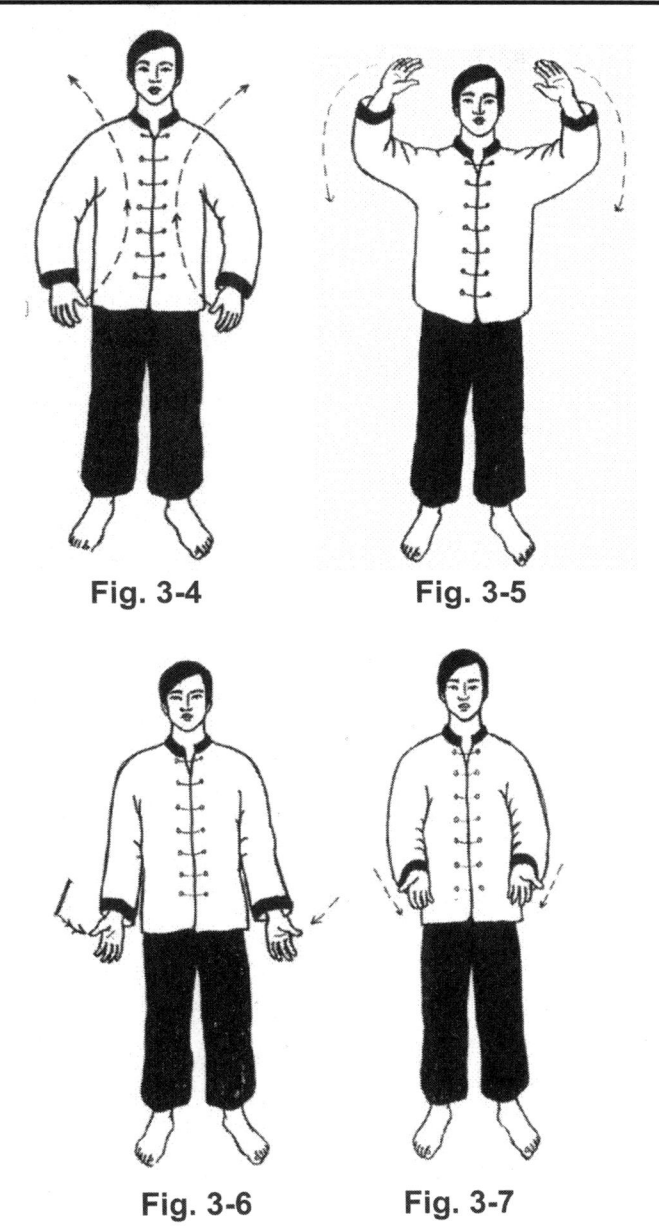

Fig. 3-5

Fig. 3-6

Fig. 3-7

B. Chi Gong Breathing

You will want to use lower abdominal breathing, so focus your attention on a point one inch below the navel. This area is known as the Lower Tan Tien (Red Planting Field). It is the source of internal power. Touch the tip of your tongue to the roof of your mouth. Inhale and exhale slowly through your nose. One breathing cycle should consist of a 3-5 second inhalation with the lower abdomen rising, holding the breath for 2-4 seconds, and then a 4-6 second exhalation as the lower abdomen sinks. With practice, the breathing cycles can grow longer, with the same ratio between inhaling, holding, and exhaling. Beginners should practice this breathing for five minutes and can gradually increase to 30 minutes or an hour.

The proper stance for this exercise should be natural and relaxed, with the feet as wide apart as the shoulders. Place the right hand over the Lower Tan Tien and cover the right hand with the left. A weak or disabled person can practice while seated on a chair or bed. See Figure 3-8 for an illustration of the stance. As you practice, you may feel warmth on the stomach and saliva may collect in your mouth. These are good indications that Chi energy is building up. Swallow the accumulated saliva slowly, about one third of the volume with each swallow.

Learning and Practicing Chi Gong 37

Fig. 3-8

C. TAOIST CLOUD PUSHING BREATHING

1. In this exercise, the wrists should remain loose and the mind focused on the Lower Tan Tien. A relaxed, slow, floating feeling should be sought.
2. Inhale and exhale through the nose.
3. Stand with your feet shoulder width apart. Hold your hands in front of your thighs with palms facing back. Inhale slowly. See Figure 3-9.
4. As you inhale, slowly raise your hands with palms down, fingers curved downward and elbows bent. See Figure 3-10.
5. Push outwards with wrists, while keeping posture straight. Make sure wrists are loose and soft with fingertips facing each other. This should be a gentle motion. Imagine that you are pressing white clouds in a blue sky. See Figure 3-11.
6. Then hold your breath as you drop your arms slowly to the beginning position. Rest focused on the Lower Tan Tien for a moment before repeating. See Figure 3-12.
7. Repeat at least 15 times. Then repeat while imagining the stored Chi energy in your Lower Tan Tien area rising up to your chest as you raise your arms. Then imagine the Chi energy radiating out through your palms as they are extended outward. After a few movements, you may begin to feel tingling and a warm sensation on your palms and fingertips. This is the sensation of Chi flow.

Fig. 3-9

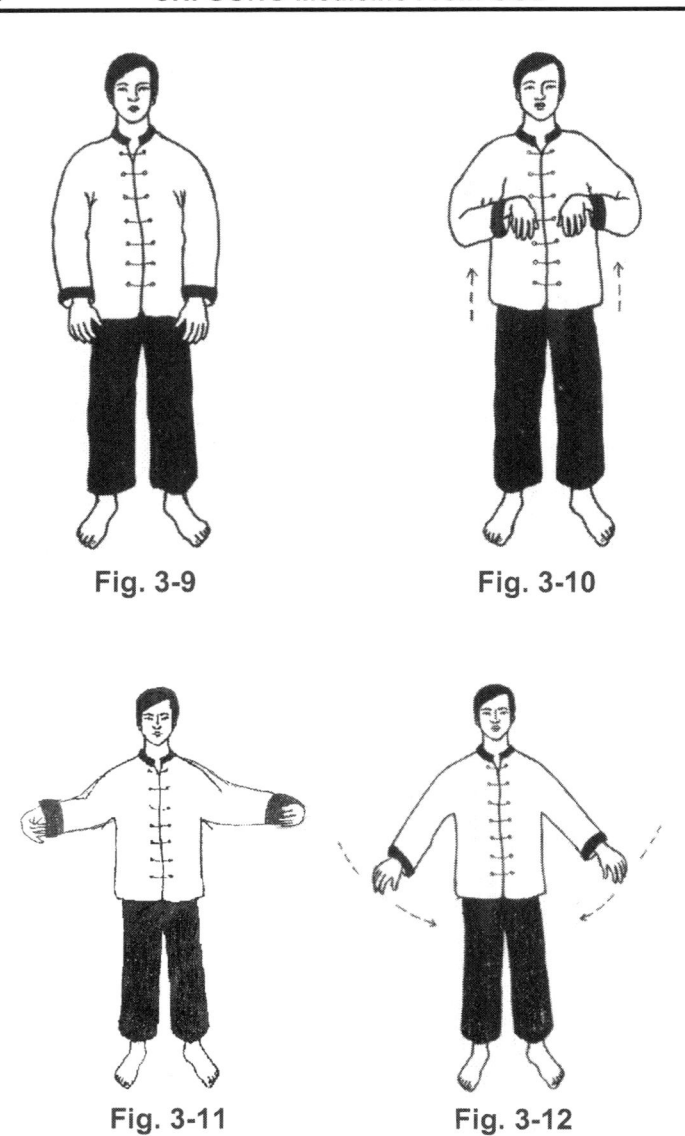

Fig. 3-10

Fig. 3-11

Fig. 3-12

Learning and Practicing Chi Gong   39

8. Close your eyes. Turn your hands so that the palms face each other as though you are holding a ball, keeping your elbows by your side. Move your hands slowly apart and together but do not touch them. You may feel that you are holding a "Chi Ball." Some people can even feel the pushing and pulling sensations of the electromagnetic wave force of Chi energy. If these three breathing exercises are practiced every day, you will sooner or later feel Chi energy yourself. See Figure 3-13.

9. Straddle a chair with your legs apart and your stomach and chest facing the chair back. First, hold your hands above the chair back with the palms facing each other and move them closer and further apart, as shown in Figure 3-14. Then rest the pinkie finger side of your wrists on the chair back as shown in Figure 3-15.

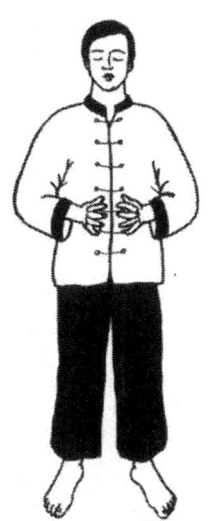

Fig. 3-13

Try to feel the Chi sensation in both cases. As you compare the sensations you feel with these two movements, you can see how Chi flow can be easily blocked even by the slight interference of resting your wrists on the chair back.

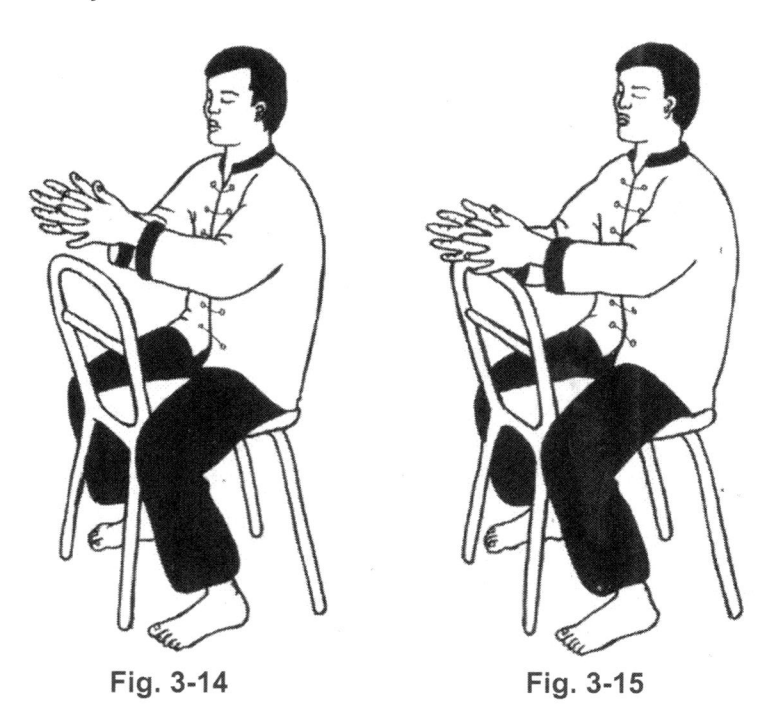

Fig. 3-14   Fig. 3-15

10. Sit on a chair facing a partner. Both of you should extend your hands with the left palm facing up and the right palm facing down. Place your right palm above your partner's left and your left palm below your partner's right palm.

    Close your eyes, touch the tip of your tongue to the roof of your mouth and breathe slowly through your nose about 100 times. Both of you will feel warmth and Chi movement. See Figure 3-16.

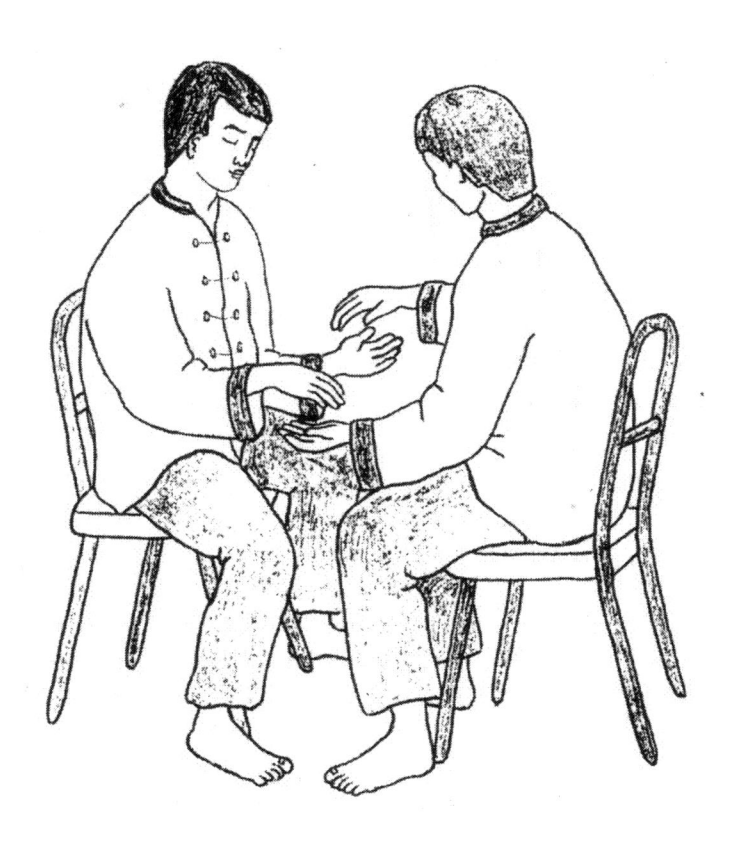

Fig. 3-16

Chi does move of its own accord, but it can also be moved by your own will power. Much of Chi Gong practice involves the control and movement of Chi. Take for example, how the simple movement in which the arms are raised in a broad inward circular motion and the palms then press down moves Chi downwards (illustrated in Figures 3-17 to 3-20).

Close your eyes and try doing this after the Chi Gong exercises a shown in figure 3-4 to 3-12. You may feel a tingling sensation in the soles of your feet when you do this, perhaps not the first time you try but certainly with enough practice. If you have a problem with one foot, you will feel it only in the other foot.

Generally, children, younger people, women and people who are sensitive will feel Chi more quickly than those who are weak, or big and muscular, or have surgery scars or have had a spinal injury. But those who have difficulty feeling Chi can feel it after a few acupuncture treatments.

The best time to practice any Chi Gong is after meditation and after having immersed your hands and feet in warm water for five minutes.

Fig. 3-17

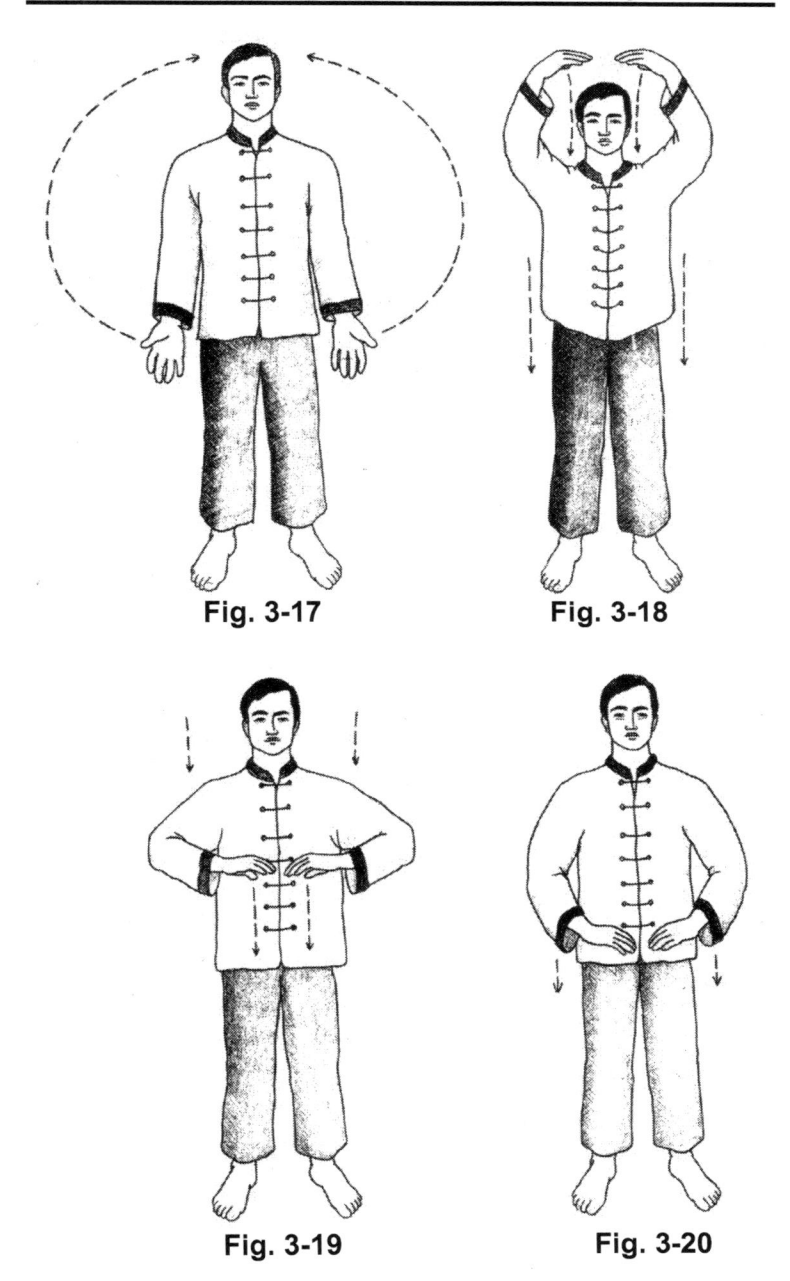

Fig. 3-18

Fig. 3-19

Fig. 3-20

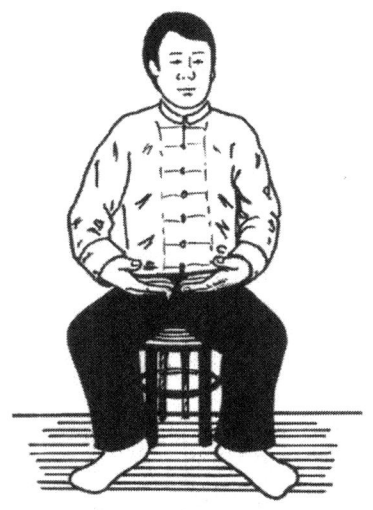

Fig. 3-21

Following is a summary of the different sounds one should make during Taoist breathing patterns as described in Figures 3-4 through 3-7, and the organ that should be vibrated by the sound. I have also included the emotion that corresponds to the breathing. Many Taoist practitioners stand in front of certain trees during the practice to address each organ. For example, for the liver, it is best to do the breathing pattern in front of a pine tree, make the shii sound, and push out your anger. People who think too much often have stomach problems, which is why they should think simple. Following is the complete chart.

Organ	**Tree**	**Sound**	**Emotion**
Liver	Pine Tree	Shii	Push out Anger
Heart	Apple Tree	Haaa	Raise up spirit
Stomach	Willow	A-Hoo	Think simple
Lung	Cypress	Th	Push out Sadness
Kidney	Cedar	Choo Wei	Push out Fear

It is taboo to do the breathing exercises in front of a peach tree. In fact, some Chinese people do not plant a peach tree in their orchard or on the side of their yard as they feel it will interfere with the spirits of their ancestors.

Why? Years ago, a monkey went up to heaven, stole and ate 3 peaches. Because the peach tree was a holy tree, he was chased by heaven's soldiers. So, a superstition developed about peach trees, which is explained in the famous Buddhist philosophy novel, "Tales of Travel to the West" written in the Ming Dynasty, 16th century.

Chi Gong Movements

First practice Zen meditation. Then, sit on a chair, with the bottom of your feet touching the ground. Place your hands on your lap, palms up, with your fingertips pointing toward each other. Inhale slowly for 5 seconds, hold your breath for 10 seconds, then exhale for 5 seconds. This is one set. Gradually increase the length of time you inhale, keeping the entire pattern in the same proportion.

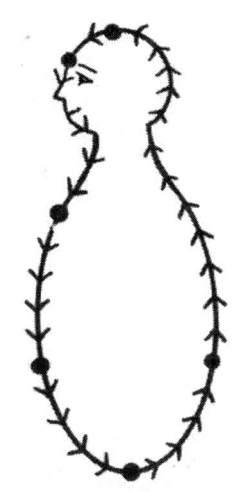

Fig. 3-22

Every third set, contract your anus muscle gently and send the chi through your spine (sacral to lumbar area). Do this for 5-10 minutes, then using the same breathing pattern, when you contract your anus on the third set, now move your Chi through up the back of your spine, over the top of your head, and down the front of your chest and abdomen to your Tan Tien, as in a circle. When you make a circle with your chi you probably will not feel it as strongly as you did when you kept it in your lumbar area (see Figure 3-22).

Fig. 3-23

Many Chi Gong practitioners stand in the horse stance and circulate their Chi as described in the second Chi movement method. To assume the horse stance posture, stand as though you are sitting on a horse, with both of your knees bent, with a straight back. Don't bend too low, it should be a few comfortable inches. Bend your arms at the elbow as if holding reins, with your fingers level at the height of the elbow. Stand in this posture and breathe for 5-10 minutes (see Figure 3-23).

Learning and Practicing Chi Gong 47

Note: The following series of movements helps the Chi flow through the channels. Refer to the diagram of acupuncture channels in Chapter 6 of this same book.

First set

While in the horse stance with regular Chi Gong breathing, bend your thumbs gradually so that they point to the floor, circulating chi through your lung channel. Slowly return the thumbs to their original position as you keep holding your breath with your anus muscle contracted. Release your breath, relax your stomach and anus muscles, then repeat with the next finger.

Next, bend your index fingers in the same way as with your thumbs, circulating your Chi through the large intestine channel. When you return these fingers to their original position, bend the second toe on each foot, circulating Chi from Stomach #1 (under the eye) through Stomach 45. Do this with each set of toes. If bending one toe is difficult at first, bend all toes together, but concentrate on the one toe you want to bend. Then, bend the big toes simultaneously, circulating Chi through the spleen channel.

Second set

Bend your small fingers and circulate the Chi through the Heart channel and the Small Intestine channel. When you return the small fingers to their original position, circulate the Chi through the Urinary Bladder channel and Kidney channel while bending your small toes.

Third set

Bend your middle fingers and circulate the Chi through the Pericardium channel. When you return the middle fingers to their original position, circulate the Chi through the Triple Warmer channel and bend the ring fingers to the floor. As you lift up the ring fingers, circulate your Chi through the Gall Bladder channel while bending your fourth toes. Then, circulate Chi through the Liver channel while bending the big toes.

Now, circulate your Chi through the Tan Tien, anus, spine, head, and chest, returning it to your Tan Tien.

Important points to note:

- People with high blood pressure, who are angry, or who suffer from heat rising to the face, like women with hot flashes, should not practice the above series. I recommend that they just circulate Chi downward, without contracting the anus muscle; practice the finger and toe bending without contracting the anus and moving the chi; or practice Buddhist style Chi Gong only.
- You can face East, face South, or follow the direction of the sun; morning to noon, face East; then from afternoon through midnight, face West.
- If you practice the horse stance more than 30 minutes, you may start to tremble. This is not due to muscle soreness, as most people first think, but from the force of the Chi meeting the gravity of the earth (electromagnetic wave force). I tell my students not to practice this stance on a cliff or while visiting the Grand Canyon, otherwise they may be pulled over!

Learning and Practicing Chi Gong

- To balance your Yin and Yang, during the day face the sun and at night face the moon. This is what Chi Gong Masters do, balance their Yin and Yang with the energy of the sun and moon.
- You should practice the series for about 30 minutes, the time it takes to circulate the chi throughout the body.
- If you practice Chi Gong at least 1-2 hours each day, you can clean up the blood in your body in just 81 days.
- Beginners should not practice with the moon for one year or more. It can disturb your sleep. This is especially true during the full moon-even if the moon is covered by clouds.

Buddhist Chi Gong

This style is very similar to Zen practice, and in fact can be describe as an extension of Zen Meditation. Compared to Taoist Chi Gong, Buddhist Chi Gong has a more spiritual aspect.

Legend says that Shakyamuni Buddha introduced 108 Zen poses, and later his disciples added more. It is interesting to note that Buddha said there are 108 worries in human life. Someone expressed this mathematically as $1^1 \times 2^2 \times 3^3 = 1 \times 4 \times 27 = 108$.

But that was 2,500 years ago. Today we need to add 3 more worries – insurance, taxes, and worrying about trying to empty the mind, or expressed mathematically, $108 + 3 = 111$.

When you practice Buddhist Chi Gong, always breath through your nose, and exhale longer than you inhale, as described in the section on Zen. Remember to limber up your body first, too. Sit on a cushion on the floor or if you have any physical limitations, sit in a chair. Look at a spot on the wall in front on you, lower than eye level. Always start with your eyes open, but if they get too sore, you can close them. Some Zen Centers and Buddhist centers insist on open eyes throughout the practice. I will not explain the different physiological or psychological differences between the two, but feel free to explore this yourself.

Buddhist Chi Gong Poses

Fig. 3-24

Figure 3-24: Sit with both palms facing forward. In this pose you can feel and exchange Chi with plants, humans, animals – even buildings and rocks. Repeat the above pose reversing the right- and left-hand positions.

Fig. 3-25

Fig. 3-25: Sit with your left palm facing heaven and your right palm facing earth. Repeat while reversing right and left-hand positions.

Fig. 3-26

Fig. 3-26: Sit with your left palm facing forward and your right palm facing the earth. Repeat with reversed right- and left-hand positions.

Fig. 3-27

Fig. 3-27: Sit with your left palm facing heaven and your right palm facing the forward. Repeat with reversed right- and left-hand positions.

Fig. 3-28

Fig. 3-28: In the prayer pose, you can send chi energy to people who live a long distance away. When you exhale, think of these people.

Fig. 3-29

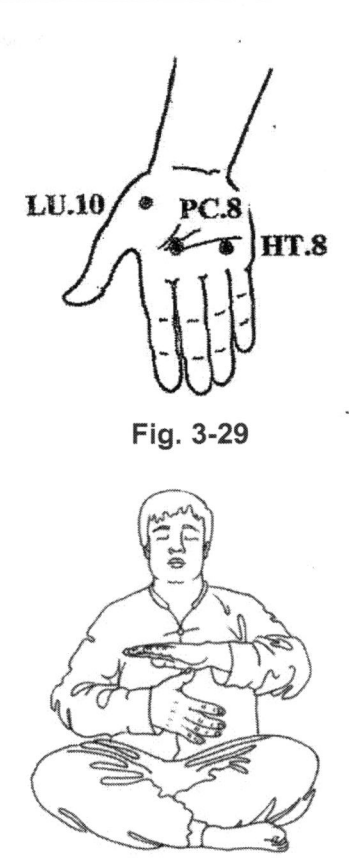

Fig. 3-30

First set: Sit with your hands as shown above, with the tip of your right thumb (Lung 11) touching Lung #10 point of your left palm near the thumb of your left palm. Circulate Chi energy through the Lung, Large Intestine, Stomach and Spleen channels. Repeat with reversed right- and left-hand positions.

Fig. 3-31

Second set   Fig. 3-31 Sit with your hands as shown above, with the tip of your right small finger (Heart #9) touching Heart #8 point on your left palm. Circulate Chi energy through Heart, Small Intestine, Urinary Bladder and Kidney channels. Repeat with reverse right- and left-hand positions.

Fig. 3-32

Third set   Fig. 3-32 Sit with your hands as shown above, with the tip of your right middle finger (Pericardium #9) touching Pericardium #8 point on your left palm. Circulate Chi energy through Pericardium, Triple Warmer, Gall Bladder and Liver channels. Repeat while reversing the right- and left-hand positions.

Additional poses

Fig. 3-33

Figs. 3-33 Sit with both hands on your knees. Use the thumb and index fingers to make a circle, but not touching. You should feel Chi flow through the tips of these fingers. You may also feel openness, acceptance, forgiveness, and peace of mind.

Fig. 3-34

The Lotus position, **Fig. 3-34**, is a common pose. Women should sit with the **left** palm touching Tan Tien and with the **right** hand over the **left**. Men should reverse the right- and left-hand positions. Worldly thoughts and a scattered mind become centered and focused, and Chi flows from Tan Tien through Du and Ren channels, or the Chi is stored in the Tan Tien. I am not able to provide additional information on the meaning of these poses. There is no book on them, and the knowledge is passed down from master to disciple. But I advise that these poses should be practiced for an extended period of time and add that these poses are dedicated to those who will reach the goal and discover their meaning.

Sue, one of my Chi Gong students, likes to imitate the hand positions of the Buddha statues in museums. You will see that there are numerous hand positions next time you go to a museum – except of course in the gift shop where they are massed produced for retail sale. On April 30, 1997, Sue was standing in front of a Buddha, encased in a glass show case and roped off, at New York's Metropolitan Museum of Art. The statue was from the Tang Dynasty (China, 618 to 907 AD.) As she imitated its hand positions, the alarm went off, much to her embarrassment. Everyone looked at her, a guard came. It was clear that she had not touched the statue or the laser surrounding it, as she was not close to it and it was roped off. You can check the security records of the museum. I fear that I am on the FBI most wanted list as I am her Chi Gong master.

Chi Gong with Talisman Symbols

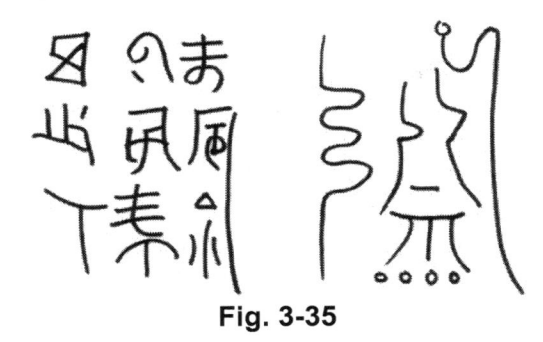

Fig. 3-35

Many people do not believe in the power of the Talisman and consider this mere superstition. But I believe that this is one of the Taoist Chi Gong methods, as it is applicable to the fundamental Taoist philosophy – anything in this world possesses both a spirit and Chi.

It is quite common for people to choose the location and direction of their house, the objects in a room, or their grave according to Feng Shui[24] (Chinese Geomancy). This is because people want to have the optimum Chi flow through their living space, and to receive help from the spirit of their ancestors.

It is interesting to note that those who have lived a non-virtuous life, like robbers, often wear a cross or Buddha around their neck because they wished to be helped by the heavenly power and want success. Clearly, Talisman symbols are used more widely than we think.

If you want to practice Talisman Chi Gong, you first need to purify your body and soul and wait for the help that will come from the heavenly spirit through the Talisman. Taoist priests or Chi Gong Masters use an existing Taoist design as a basis and add to it based on an individual's needs. It is similar to a Yogi or Guru who makes a special mantra for a disciple.

Before writing a Talisman, a Taoist priest will clean his room, take a bath with cold water, leave a bowl of clean water at the back of his house, bow to the East, West, South and North, spit out a mouthful of water, bite his teeth three times, bring the water back into his room, straighten his clothes, light a candle, pray to God or a Spirit, and write a Talisman. If the client of a Taoist priest uses a regular solar calendar with regard to time of birth, the priest will convert this information into a lunar calendar. The priest will write the Talisman on white or yellow paper, or on a board made from a peach tree, using red ink or red cinnabar. He will then give his blessing and chi to the Talisman.

Herbal Chi Gong

Herbal Chi Gong Prescription
Ren Shen, Radix Ginseng - Asian Ginseng Root.6 grams
Gan Cao, Radix Glycyrrhizae – Licorice Root-----6 grams
Bai Zhu, Rhizoma Atractylodis Alba……………...9 grams
Dang Gui, Radix Angelica Sinsensis – Angelica Root…..
……9 grams
Chuan Xiong, Rhizoma Ligustici Wallichii ………..6 grams
Shu Di Huang, Radix Rehmanniae - cooked Rehmannia Root…………………….…..9 grams
Bai Shao, Radix Paeoniae Albae - White Peony Root
……6 grams
Fu Ling, Poria Cocos, tuckhoe, hoelen…………..9 grams

This formula is good for Chi Gong or internal style martial arts and also for one who practices an external style of martial arts or sports.

First Month
One hour after taking the pill, lie down on your back. Gently rub your palms on your stomach area from your navel to solar plexus area, from the right side to the left side, then from the left side to the right side. Concentrate on your palms and rid yourself of worldly thoughts. You will feel sleepy. Do this 3 times a day, 15-20 minutes at a time, and after you have finished, practice Zen meditation for 10-30 minutes.

Second Month
Complete the first month's procedure as described above. After you move your palms along your stomach area, squeeze the muscles in this area, and make a fist. Softly hit your stomach area with your fist. Then, with a small wooden hammer, softly hit your stomach area and ribs.

Third Month
Repeat the procedure outlined for the second month above. With the wooden hammer, hit the side of your rib area, then rub this area with your palms.

Fourth Month
Same procedure as in the third month.

Fifth - Eight Months
Repeat the procedure for the third month and then, for men, rub your chest and shoulder with your palms, hit with a wooden hammer, and rub again with your palms; women should only massage their breasts. This will develop chi flow through the front part of your body and the Ren Channel.

Ninth - Twelfth Months
Lie down on your stomach. With the appropriate palm, rub from your right shoulder to below your neck. Next, from your left shoulder to below the neck, then from your neck to the lumbar area through your spine and then to the

sacral area. Then, repeat with the wooden hammer.

For the next part of the exercise, turn over and rub the front part of your body with your palm, then use the wooden hammer. As with the other months, practice Zen afterwards.

After one year, you will feel tremendous Chi energy flow through your body, especially through the Ren and Du channels.

Chanting Chi Gong

When you practice Taoist and Buddhist types of Chi Gong, you may feel warmth and Chi energy flow through your stomach area and then your chest, or through your kidney area along the back side of your body. You may also feel heaviness or trembling between your eyes (the third eye spot). These sensations may appear within a few months or years, depending on the individual and how much he/she is dedicated to practice.

I am able to open the third eye of my students, but it can sometimes make them nervous, dizzy, or even make them vomit. Why? The Chi flow is often not smooth for city dwellers. If the third eye is well developed, it is not uncommon for a color picture to appear in front of the third eye or for a student to dream in vibrant colors. Sometimes one can predict the future when the third eye is open or see a past event or former life. Telepathic powers can also be developed when the third eye is open.

To chant, you should assume one of the positions described in the Zen meditation instructions. The Chi flow in this form of Chi Gong is opposite of that of Taoist Chi Gong – in this case, the chi flows from the universe, God, or any spirit or tangible or intangible object through the top of your head (Du20). It then flows downward through your spine to your anus, and up through the Tan Tien (navel area).

When you give Chi energy to others, you should not chant out loud, rather only to yourself (in your mind), to God, Moses, Jesus, Buddha, Mohammed or Allah. Chi energy will come through your head, so you do not draw upon the energy stored in your Tan Tien.

As with other practices, this takes time and effort to achieve results. You need to be spiritually cleaned and pure to channel the energy from God or even the Devil. People with very weak heart energy should start with Chanting.

The top of the head (Du#20 point) is like a satellite TV antenna. It will channel many interesting color dreams or nightmares whether or not this spot is clear (no pain on pressure) or blocked.

When you chant in a quiet place in a meditation pose, you call "Holy Spirit," "Moses," "Jesus," "Buddha," "Mohammed" or "Allah." When you exhale with or without sound, you repeat the name of whom you called for 30 minutes. Later you may feel warmth come though your head and down along your spine, or you may feel heaviness in your head or dizziness.

Beginners often feel it even a few hours later. If you practice chanting in a quiet place, such as in the mountains or in the desert from midnight until 4 a.m., just before dawn you might scream, jump, or pull out a big tree because you have received too much Chi energy.

I recommend chanting to cancer patients who are weak, old, or not able to perform ordinary Chi Gong breathing exercises. I also recommend chanting to those who heal others, if they get tired when giving Chi to their patients.

If you visit a Buddhist temple, you will see many priests who read canons out loud. Their voices come from their Tan Tien area, not from their throats, or from vibrating throats. The priests employ this method to build up Chi energy by forceful breathing, to get rid of worldly thoughts while reciting the canon, and to summon the author's spirit.

I met a Buddhist priest who can call and gather spirits of the dead then exorcise to get rid of them by chanting. It was an eerie experience, as he could fill up an entire valley with the ghost spirits, even in the daytime.

I highly recommend the chanting method of Chi Gong to people with heart problems and schizophrenic patients who show symptoms similar to those of one who is possessed, because these patients have difficulty practicing regular Chi Gong breathing exercises.

One thing comparable to chanting is talking in tongues (glossolalia) in Pentecostal of other Christian Churches in America. The members of the congregation sing a hymn aloud and yell a word like "Jesus," or "Holy Spirit." Suddenly people start talking in tongues. Usually, their language is not used in the present time or anywhere on earth. Some may channel the voice of Buddha or of Jesus as it was during his life.

Several Korean Shamans are able to make the same voice as the dead, whether man or woman, old or young, and speak from the dead person's memory, even though they never met the deceased. Most of these are women who are possessed by a spirit.

Perhaps someone claimed a Chi Gong master visited your area for a few days or you visit a Chi Gong center for training. Sometimes, besides meditation, breathing exercise, and Tai Chi movements, a chanting session can be added for long hours. You may receive energy from God, Buddha, Moses or Mohammed. Satan or another evil spirit may provide evil words. Make sure you know what you are chanting in a foreign language. They may say the chanting words are for God, but it may be from Satan. If unwanted symptoms occur in your body, you cannot easily contact the master. Therefore, you should go to an established place with a good reputation.

Fasting

The history of fasting is so ancient that no one can determine its exact date of origin. In Korean mythology, about 5,000 years ago, a female bear and tiger fasted and prayed for 100 days in a cave, desiring to be human. They ate only garlic and mugwort leaves. The Tiger had no patience and gave up. Only the bear succeeded and became a woman. She bore a son who became the first king of the Korean kingdom, Dan Gun.

A chief, a medicine man, or a shaman of Native Americans, used to fast in a cave, desert, or wilderness for many days, to receive inspiration from God. Yogis and Taoists usually fast for 30, 40, or 100 days. Moses fasted for 40 days at the top of Sinai Mountain, without water or food, as told in the Old Testament of the Bible. More than 21 days is the quickest way to achieve the highest level of Chi Gong – that is, to receive inspiration from God. A man could become a religious leader or holy figure in this way, but why was there no woman who has been able to reach this phase throughout the history of the world? If a woman fasts for more than a week, it has to be within a group, otherwise she could be possessed by an evil spirit or never wake up as a "normal" person. While it is true that there are more psychic women than men, the highest level has always been reached by a man, who is capable of fasting for long periods alone.

At Ameipa, a Taoist woman's group in China, they practice the Taoist religion, rituals, ceremonies and Chi Gong. They sometimes fast, but always in a group. My female Chi Gong students said they would like to challenge the man's world. But this challenge would need to take place alone and in a cave. I cannot guarantee that I will be able exorcise them if they return and possessed by an evil spirit or plagued with madness. There are so many equal opportunities for women these days. And who knows? Maybe New England will produce the first woman religious leader in the history of **wo**mankind. Maybe it will be one of my students.

While fasting in the desert, you should spread cow skin on the sand just before dawn to collect the dew to drink. When the Korean Tiger troops fought in the Vietnam War in 1965, some of them had active duty as radiomen on top of the hill. They were supposed to receive a supply of water from U.S. Army helicopters, but often there was too much gun fire from the Viet Cong soldiers for them to land. During the 6-month dry season, there was no rain at all, and creeks dried up. The Korean soldiers were able to combat their thirst by spreading their rain ponchos on the grass to collect the dew before dawn.

If an earthquake occurred in Los Angeles, California, seven million would potentially suffer from thirst and a large portion could die from dehydration. So, the population was taught survival techniques, and instructed to carry a plastic trash bag in the car. This could be used as a blanket while sleeping on the ground and would collect the dew for drinking upon waking up.

I like to recommend a diet or that my clients reduce their daily intake of food while on a daily job schedule but if one wants a more spiritual experience besides losing weight, one should go to a quiet spot, like a mountain, a sanatorium or a Zen center.

One should practice Chi Gong breathing exercises regularly at least one hour per day for 30 days before dieting or 100 days before a few days of diet or fasting. You should not practice Chi Gong if you are plagued by extreme worry or anxiety over things like divorce, bankruptcy, or chronic and/or severe illness.

Fasting (Diet) with Seaweed

If you have a serious, acute disease, or have been weakened by chronic illness, you should not fast. If you are diabetic, have experienced heart or kidney failure, stomach ulcers, ulcerative colitis, lung problems such as asthma, cancer, or mental illness, it is imperative that you consult with your Western physician and then with an experienced teacher of fasting. Depending upon the degree of your medical problems, you can undertake a fasting regime. In fact, I have helped many patients successfully treat their disease through fasting taught at my center or on retreat.

Before undertaking this program, you should have your physician check your stool for traces of parasites, and if you test positive, receive a prescription. You should start your medication a week before fasting.

I typically recommend one or two days of fasting for beginners. You can consume only water, but I recommend a soup with seaweed and mushroom.

Five days prior to your fast
DO NOT EAT MEAT OR MEAT-BASED SOUPS – eat soups that are from easily digestible foods.

5th day before fasting – consume 1/2 of normal food intake
4th day before fasting – consume 1/2 of normal food intake
3rd day before fasting – consume 1/3 of normal food intake
2nd day before fasting – consume 1/3 of normal food intake
Day before fasting – consume 1/4 of normal food intake

Fasting program
First day of fast –
    Drink water only– no tea. Drink 2 to 3 liters or ½ to 2/3 gallon of water with 1 gram of potassium, 5 grams of salt and 3 grams of magnesium added.
    Noon – seaweed soup

    Evening – seaweed soup

Second day of fast –
    Take a laxative in the morning. Drink water only– no tea.
    Noon – seaweed soup
    Evening – seaweed soup
    or
Second day of fast – 1/4 of regular food intake

After your fast has been completed:
1st day after fasting – consume 1/4 of normal food intake.
2nd day after fasting – consume 1/3 of normal food intake
3rd day after fasting – consume 1/2 of normal food intake

4th day after fasting – consume 1/2 of normal food intake
5th day after fasting – consume 1/2 of normal food intake
6th day after fasting – consume 2/3 of normal food intake
7th day after fasting – back to normal food intake

Notes: It is a good idea to take the parasite medicine as if you have them. For, if you fast, they could penetrate the stomach or intestinal wall if they get hungry, causing pain and trouble. The special seaweed, mushroom and herbal soup will make you less hungry during your fast. After you complete your fast, you must follow the food schedule. If you take too much food too soon, your shrunken stomach won't be able to handle it and you will experience pain and discomfort. If you take laxatives on the second day, you will have dark, smelly feces – an indication of cleansing your stomach and intestinal wall.

After you have completed the fasting program, you can use the seaweed and mushroom soup as part of your diet program with much success. If you like, you can add other ingredients, such as sugar to suit your taste.

<u>Basic Fasting Formula</u>
15 g (1/2 oz) dried mushroom
15 g (1/2 oz) seaweed
5 pieces of date
10 grams of licorice
One or two tablespoons of soy sauce
One quart of water

Soak the mushroom and seaweed for 24 hours prior to preparing; discard the water and rinse. (Note: herbs used in the formula should not be soaked.) Boil for about 20 minutes, then simmer 30 minutes. Other herbs can be added based on an individual's condition.

Take half of this soup twice a day, or four times a day with two packs, eat mushrooms and seaweed. if you do not like soy sauce, omit that. If you do not like the taste of licorice, then replace it with sugar or nothing else, at all. Be sure to include 5 grams of salt per day.

During prolonged periods of fasting, it is common for most people's skin and gums to become weaker. It is important not to brush your teeth hard, which you might tend to due to get rid of the unwanted bad smell from fasting. Since your facial skin will probably get softer, you should shave lightly if at all. When you shower or bathe, use lukewarm water – hot water may burn your skin. You might need to wear more layers of clothing as you may feel colder than usual. You may also sweat more.

During the fast, you should read some good books. Also, I recommend that fasting practitioners have at least one month of Chi Gong training, before fasting. Also, during fasting you should practice Zen meditation and Buddhist Chi Gong.

If unwanted symptoms appear during or after fasting, such as stomach pain, rashes or emotional problems, see a physician immediately and gradually increase your food intake according to the schedule.

While fasting, your Zen practice will be easier, and you will feel pureness and tranquility more than during your normal eating times. You may even get a taste of nirvana!

I suggest that you fast once or twice a year, or even every season. You can increase each fasting period by 2-3 days. If you fast more than 5 days at a time, then I strongly urge you to go to a center which specializes in the art of fasting, one with a quiet environment.

Throughout your lifetime, you should keep good diet habits. I do not recommend a strict vegetarian diet for most people under 25 years of age, or those who live in a cold climate. Hindus in India, and those in Uganda of Africa are vegetarians because the climate is warm. Otherwise, a long-term vegetarian diet can cause a Yang deficiency – symptoms include a cold body, sluggishness, no vitality, etc. Women's menstrual cycles may come over more than 30, 32, 35, or even more days. Menstrual cycles may even be skipped for months. Only Taoist, Buddhists and Chi Gong Masters who practice Chi Gong regularly will not experience these symptoms if they are vegetarians. I myself eat mostly vegetables, whole grain rice, fish, beans, fruits, tofu (bean curd), sesame oil, and seaweed soup.

I highly recommend a day of fasting if you catch a cold. It is interesting to note that when animals are sick, such as poisoned by a snake bite, then do not eat or drink for two or three days until they fully recover. Animals can hibernate but most humans cannot – the exceptions are a few Yogis and Taoists who are capable of short periods of hibernation.

When most Taoists fast, they try to take care of their body, by taking a small amount of food. Buddhists can fast 7, 21 or 49 days even today. But even a Buddhist priest can die from 49 days of fasting, although they can reach the nirvana state and die happy! Buddhist priests can stay in a cave or even in a small room as small as 100 square feet. Sometimes it is sealed with rocks and clay, leaving only a small hole like a jail cell so they can have food passed in and send out feces. Some stay there for a year or even more to read Buddhist texts or practice Zen meditation or both.

Most Korean Buddhist sects put an equal value on Zen and texts. One can study either one first or both at the same time.

It is good to first study texts to learn about life and the guidelines, then practice Zen. The former is Yang and the latter is Yin. Both need to be balanced.

Jesus and Shakyamuni Buddha fasted even though they had learned enough of the philosophy of life through books and teachers. When Jesus was 15 years-old he discussed the Old Testament with Bible scholars, Rabbis and priests. But he fasted 40 or more days to enlighten himself.

The tradition of American Christianity began during colonial times. A pastor prayed, taught and preached the Bible to the settlers and soldiers, most of whom were illiterate. The tradition of meditation and praying for long hours and days by Catholic fathers, nuns and pastors was diminished after the crossing of the Atlantic Ocean. Pentecostal and Gospel music styles are becoming increasingly popular among American Christians these days.

A Buddhist or Taoist goes to a quite place like the mountains or a temple for a retreat to meditate, practice Zen, pray, fast, or be silent (not talk) for days. Most American Christians' daily retreat schedules are filled with preaching, singing hymns, campfires, games and sports. It is more of a social rather than a religious gathering.

Settlers and pilgrims would have done well to have learned fasting and meditation from the medicine men of the Native Americans. Instead, some shot them with guns, gave them alcohol, and subjected them to the first biological warfare in mankind's history, whether they knew it or not, by giving them contaminated blankets from sick and dying soldiers. There are also some accounts of shaman/medicine men having their legs cut off!

The world's greatest spiritual leaders, men like Jesus Christ, Moses, Buddha, Mohammed, and Yogi, and the ancient Taoist monks all practiced similar forms of fasting meditation during their lives for 30, 40, or even 100 days at a time. Even today, on the outskirts of Beijing, China, there are military special forces training schools where trainees fast in caves for twenty-one days, learning Chi Gong meditation and sharpening their perceptual skills.

North Korean spies are also trained in this way, which enables them to feel the presence of humans or even small animals like rabbits in the darkness at a distance of 100 meters. Using only this special technique developed through meditation and fasting. Their senses are so acute that they can detect buried land mines. With these skills they can infiltrate the heavily guarded border between North and South Korea.

But, within two years after coming to the South, these spies can lose the ability to use their special training and they may even find that their normal sensory functions like hearing sight, and smell have become impaired. This is due to the fact that they can no longer continue the Taoist Chi Gong meditation that they had practiced in the mountains of North Korea.

During the war in Viet Nam, it was very difficult to capture Viet Cong officers. Many had been trained at the military special forces training school near Beijing where they learned martial arts and Ninja skills. When pursued, they knew how to hide under water and breathe through reeds. They could also plaster themselves with mud and leaves and lie motionless to camouflage themselves when they were in danger of detection. Yet, they sometimes met their match in the South Korean Tiger troops. The South Koreans were forbidden to use any substances containing scents, from coffee and cigarettes to deodorant and toothpaste, which might give a clue to their presence. When they hid in ambush, they not only caught Viet Cong soldiers but were actually able to hunt and kill approaching tigers. What sort of training must these Tiger troops have had to be able to successfully apprehend the Viet Cong?

Martial arts movies have become very popular over the years and by. Now probably everyone is familiar with Ninjas from Japanese samurai movies or their equivalents in Chinese and Korean films. They camouflage their faces with black cloth and cover their bodies with black suits. Then they infiltrate their enemies' strongholds on espionage or assassination missions.

Sometimes they are shown communicating with each other while they are hiding without being heard by the other people in the room. This is not simply a cinematic device.

Someone who has received true Ninja training has developed auditory skills much sharper than those of ordinary humans. Like many animals they are able to hear sounds of much lower frequencies than the average person.

Using their heightened senses, they are also able to detect from a distance how many of their enemies are in hiding, whether outdoors in a forest, or on the other side of a thick wall. They are even able to see the spirits of dead people and ghosts. Training to develop such extraordinary skill originated in India, Tibet, and China long ago, and was exported to Japan via Korea.

Praying

People of all religions pray to their god as part of their belief. Sculptors for Buddhist temples ate a vegetarian diet and took a bath each day, with cold water even during the winter. They also did not have sex or argue with anyone in order to clean and purify their body and soul for 21 or 100 days before beginning their work. This tradition and custom was passed down voluntarily for thousands of years without the supervision of a priest.

Korean women prayed to God or a spirit in heaven, the earth, in mountains, or in the water to help prevent sickness, or help their business, farming or fishing by putting a bowl of clean water on a small table in the back yard at night.

When my mother's cousin was in her late 40's, her husband was captured by the Communist and her elder son joined the military as a volunteer when in high school. During the Korean war, she lived through a cold winter in the southern province as a refugee. She bathed with cold water and prayed for 100 days. On the 101st day, when she went to the market, she saw many young men who looked like homeless men. One was her son. She was fortunate – many student soldiers died from frost bite and starvation during that time.

A group of people called "Simmani" who seek and gather natural ginseng root in Korean mountains follow a similar regime. They bathe every day, eat a vegetarian diet, are celibate, and pray for 21 days, or longer, so they can receive inspiration or a message during sleep or in a dream from the mountain spirit. When they climb into the mountains, they speak softly out of respect to the mountain and its spirit. Sometimes they may find a wild ginseng root 100 years old, worth more than $10,000 in U.S. dollars.

I recall back in 1954 when I was in elementary school, a 40-year-old couple prayed for a baby in the mountain area of the Eastern province of Korea. One night, a mountain spirit, (usually an old man with a white beard), wearing a white robe, appeared in the woman's dream and told her to go to a certain spot in the mountains. There she found a baby-shaped and similarly sized ginseng root more than 100 years old which was of immeasurable value. This she received instead of a pregnancy. This story was in the newspapers, as are many similar stories today

When you pray, it is important to clean the body and forgive someone that you have argued with. It is important to remember that you must not only clean and purify your body, but also, your soul before you pray

Chi Gong and Zen Differences

Throughout my career, I have been asked by many to answer this question, "What is the difference between Chi Gong and Zen?" There is no book that I am aware of that mentions this. But what I think is that the purpose of Chi Gong is to build chi energy, while the purpose of Zen is to attain tranquility and peace of mind.

Holding the breath is the main part of Taoist style Chi Gong; inhaling and exhaling longer is Buddhist style. In both, the tongue touches the roof of the mouth, just behind the back of the two center front teeth. As discussed in the beginning of this book, when I teach Taoist style Chi Gong class, after the warm-up exercises, we practice Zen style – not touching the tongue to the roof of the mouth – by breathing in an out, for 5 to 10 minutes. Then we start Chi Gong. We do not practice this Zen breathing before Buddhist-style Chi Gong, as there is no need – they both achieve the same results. If one practices Zen-style many hours per day for many years, or one practices just sitting

Chi Gong for the same time period, the goal is the same, namely, to achieve peace of mind and to free the flow of Chi energy and build up Chi.

The Speed of Chi Energy

Albert Einstein, the scientist famous for his theory, $E=MC^2$, believed that light had weight and could be pulled by gravity. He also stated that the only constant measuring device in the universe is the speed of light.

Then, what is the speed of Chi energy? Is it the same as the speed of light? When we exchange Chi energy in class with other class members (see Figure 3-14) and send Chi even a long distance. It seems that it has volume and speed.

When God, the Creator, gives us inspiration, healing power, messages or responds to our prayers, it takes no time. Whether we live 1,000 light years from anyone, or communicate with extra-terrestrials, or God, who sends Chi energy to us, it does not take time, like the speed of light takes time to reach us. Why? Chi energy is beyond our 3-dimensional world, it is not comprehended by ordinary human beings. It is infinite.

Then why would someone's Chi energy reach long distances and others' not? It depends on several things: Is the receiver sensitive or pure in his/her body and mind? Does the receiver have the will to receive this energy? Does the sender have a large amount of Chi energy, so that what is sent is more like a truck rather than a bicycle? While both large and small amounts of Chi energy will reach a place with the same speed, the impact will be different. But if many bicycles of Chi go together the impact will be noticeable. That is why many people pray together to heal a patient.

When two people exchange chi energy as in Figure 3-16, it feels as though there is an Electro-magnetic field, a pulling or pushing feeling. So, it would seem that this current can be disturbed by another object, as are light and electric waves. But this is not the case with chi energy. It can reach anywhere in the universe at any time, past, present, or future, with the same force if there is no interference from evil – because it is beyond our 3-dimensional existence.

How to Lose Weight Using Chi Gong Breathing Techniques

Clasp hands together under navel while making a short breath with a little bit of air with the bottom part of the stomach bulging out. Then, push hands together up towards the chest putting air into the chest while shrinking the stomach, pushing with two palms. Hold air there as long as possible. Put air down to the stomach internally.

Then, exhale through mouth a long breath like "shhhhhhhhhh" like a whistle. Shrink the stomach even more and after the air is all exhaled, make a sound with "poo poo poo" through the mouth with tension of upper stomach muscle to release the last few breaths in the air. Try this ten times three times a day as long as you can.

Cold Temperature and Cold Drinks Increases Body Weight

People drink cold soda, water, eat ice cream, and use air conditioners to cool the room temperature during the summer. While our brain knows that it is summer when the air conditioner is on, our body responds to the cool air and cold food as if it were winter, and stores food in the form of fat deposits. This is our natural inclination to store food to use for energy and insulation during cold weather, and we typically store this fat in the stomach area. It stands to reason, then, that if you want to lose weight and fat deposits from your stomach area, that you should avoid eating cold foods & using air conditioners.

It is better to consume water at room temperature year-round. It is interesting to note that American restaurants serve ice water to customers. It is an accepted, yet not proven hypothesis, that cold temperatures trigger the production of a digestive enzyme that makes us hungry. It has also been observed that school children eat more snacks on a cool, rainy day than a sunny day. This may be due to psychological reasons.

Bellows Breathing

First, rub both your hands and feet for five minutes, or, to warm up your feet more than your hands, immerse your feet in warm to hot water for five minutes; this will also warm up your stomach area by helping Chi to flow.

Second, cover the stomach area with one palm over the other, and inhale though your nose faster than normal breathing speed, filling up the lungs and lower diaphragm and bulging your stomach area. Then push into your stomach forcefully with both palms to push air out through your mouth with any one of the five organ-vibrating sounds as described in the section of Taoist Chi Gong Breathing exercises. Do these 100 or more times, two-three times a day. For one or two hundred days, and you will lose weight and flatten your stomach area. You will also get more Chi energy.

If you practice reverse breathing techniques, inhaling to shrink your stomach and exhaling to make it bulge, it will massage your internal organs, as in Yogi breathing. This is also good for practitioners of martial arts as it toughens up the body internally and externally. Reverse breathing will make your stomach bulge up with abundant Chi energy like Bodhidharma.

Animal or Plant Kingdom: Which One Lives Longer?

The oldest tree lived 5,000 years. So, we must imitate the tree. We should pretend to stand like a tree.

Fig. 3-36 **Fig. 3-37**

- Both the Yin part of the body (ventral) and the palms facing the sun. (Fig.3-36)

- Both the Yang part of the body (Dorsal) and dorsal part of the hand facing the sun. (Fig.3-37)

You do not have to face sun directly. Bend your knee slightly and touch the tip of your tongue to the roof of your mouth and breathe through the nose as in basic Chi Gong breathing. One who can stand it for longer hours, will get more Chi - one, two or maybe even three hours? Start with 10 minutes.

The turtle or the leopard - which one lives longer?

Turtles! Turtles move slowly and breathe very slowly. So, they live 200 years.

Fig. 3-38

1. Korean Martial Art Chi Gong (Fig.3-38)

Sit on the floor with a cushion or sit on a chair. First inhale a small amount of air similar to when you sit and read a book or study. Push the air down with mild force to your lower abdomen. Hold the air for 10 seconds. Push more air down with sharp tension with a short "Um" sound. Air should not escape much from your mouth. Hold your breath for two more seconds and then exhale through the nose for 10 seconds. Repeat it 10 times for a set. This is more like martial art training type Chi Gong. You can repeat 3 sets per one hour class. Between set intervals do another sit on type Buddhist Chi Gong practice.

2. Korean Heat Chi Gong

When I was living in Boston, Massachusetts. My studio had heated wooden floors and advanced students would sometimes cover their heads with a thick towel and wear a hooded sweatshirt, thick long pants and socks and do the previous breath holding method. A few minutes later, they would have much sweat and sometimes their teeth would start to hit together with a light trembling. The by-product is a large amount of lost weight and gaining tremendous Chi energy. However, losing weight is not the purpose of this Chi Gong. This type of Chi Gong is not as comfortable mentally compared to Buddhist Chi Gong. This procedure is very uncomfortable; therefore, it is better for a martial artist. It requires tremendous endurance.

3. One will gather Chi energy by doing as written at the beginning of this book and by using this method.

Close your eyes. Rub both hands and then slap together. (Fig 3-39), (Fig.3-40).

Fig. 3-39   **Fig.3-40**

Fig.3-41

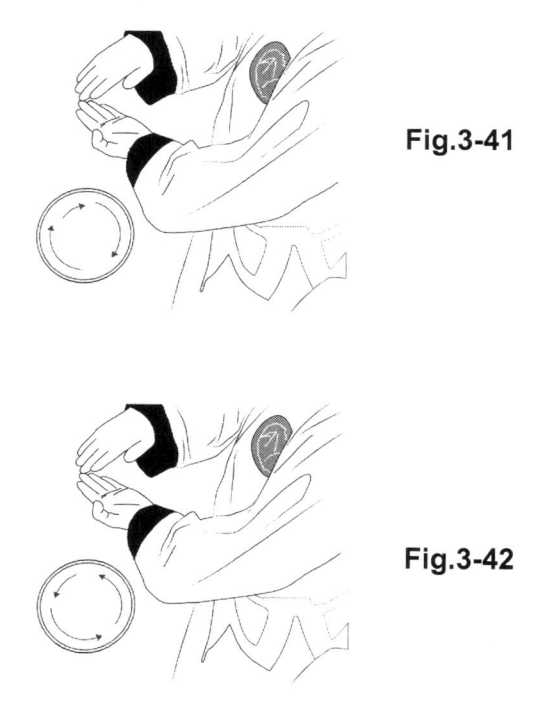

Fig.3-42

Then, put right palm over left palm without touching. Make 100 circles in each direction - right palm clockwise (Fig.3-41) and then counterclockwise 100 times. (Fig.3-42)

Do you feel the difference? Young children, teenagers and women are more sensitive than men or people over 50 years old. There are always exceptional people over 70 years old that may still feel the Chi flow. Gay men are sometimes like women, they are more sensitive than ordinary men. If one feels more Chi energy while moving counterclockwise than clockwise, it is a good indication of super sensitivity. The earth rotates counterclockwise and revolves around the Sun in the same direction.

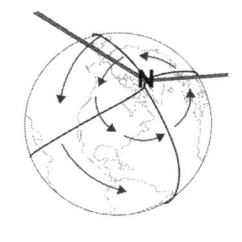

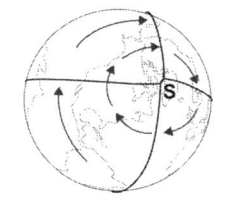

(Fig. 3-43)   (Fig. 3-44)

4. Earth Rotations

When you are in a rocket and flying thru under the earth and you look up the earth, it turns clockwise as you look at the glove model (Fig.3-44). If you want to give Chi energy to the other astronaut, you should turn your hands clockwise. If you are in middle of the galaxy, you should check the individual stars to figure it out. It depends upon your perspective. Astronomers said that about half of the galaxies rotate counterclockwise and the other half of them rotate clockwise. Also, some galaxies are perpendicular or at different angles to the Milky Way galaxy. I guess that the Sun and the Milky Way galaxy are considered as a datum point and plane. All galaxies on the same level or under appeared to rotate counterclockwise and other galaxies on the above the Sun and Milky way galaxy may appeared to rotate clockwise. If a rocket flies above all the galaxies and looks down, it may appear to rotate counterclockwise but, if the rocket flies underneath the galaxies and looks up, it may appear to rotate clockwise. The perspective of the turning direction of the stars and galaxies are affected by your location. Furthermore, if one feels more added energy counterclockwise and energy moves out clockwise, know that there are a very few super sensitive people who can cultivate Chi easier than other ordinary people. Look at perspective of where you are.

84 **CHI GONG Medicine From GOD**

Athletes run counterclockwise on Olympic racing and ice-skating rink tracks, even horse and car racing in the U.S. But some European countries do horse and car racing clockwise.

Ancient Greek chariot racing required the chariot to stay on the left side of the track and rotate counterclockwise. So, the rider could pull out his weapon with his right hand. Similarly, Japanese samurais walk on a street on their left side so they can pull out a sword easily with their right hand.

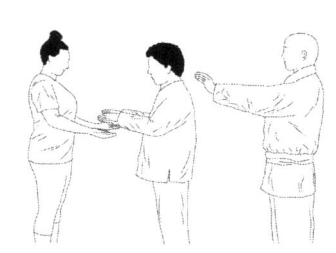

Fig. 3-45   Fig 3-46

5. Chi Energy

A (Fig.3-45) shows Master Kim giving Chi energy to a closed eyed student.

B (Fig.3-46) shows Master Kim giving Chi energy to a student while another student sends Chi through his palm close to the scapula area of Master Kim.

The Chi receiving student will suddenly feel more Chi energy. This is because she got energy from two batteries. If there are more students involved, she will get much more energy. Many religious sects do group prayer for a person or a specific group of people throughout the history of the world.

Learning and Practicing Chi Gong 85

Fig. 3-47

6. Sending Chi

Chi energy is not easily understood by ordinary people. It works differently as in a different dimension. It will not only penetrate a wall but, it can also transmit through many walls and at any distance. (Fig. 3-47)

I can demonstrate this to a group of students while I am standing three walls away from the students and sending Chi energy thru walls. A witness standing in the middle of us on the corridor can observe when I send Chi energy thru the wall. Close-eyed students respond by moving their hand. Sometimes I demonstrate through other connected stores in the same building with 20 walls.

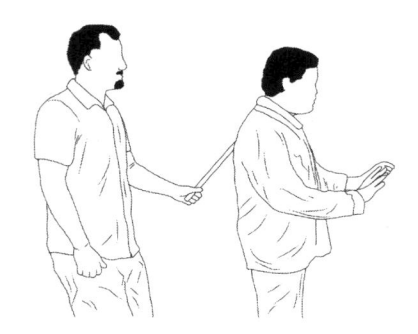

Fig. 3-48

Fig. 3-49

I can send Chi energy a long distance and this has been witnessed by telephone. It is not Chi sending through the telephone. A witness person answers the phone and hears my sound when I send Chi to the receiving person with closed eyes and responds to it by moving the fingers. The success rate is 90 percent. (Fig.3-48) (Fig.3-49) I did it from Oklahoma City, Oklahoma to Boston, MA. This is a

Learning and Practicing Chi Gong 87

distance of 1,750 miles. It works in different dimensions. It works by your noble intention. Your will power can move Chi energy to any-where in the Universe.

How to Deliver Baby Easily

Please watch instruction video with above title
www.kwangmooryu.com

First, the mother must do Chi Gong breathing for a few minutes. A Doctor, nurse, midwife or her husband should do finger massage lightly 30 times to the following points. For acupuncture point locations, look on the internet.

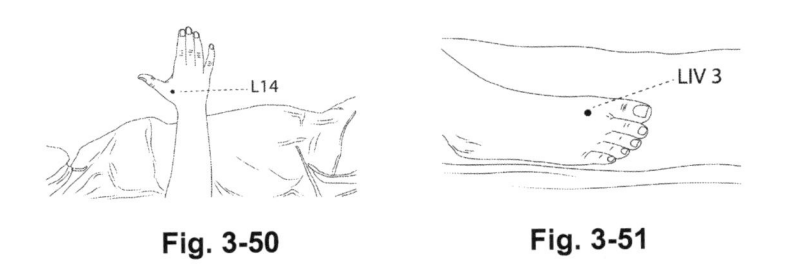

Fig. 3-50   **Fig. 3-51**

Large Intestine #4 - Acupuncture point (Fig. 3-50).
Liver #3 Acupuncture - point (Fig. 3-51)

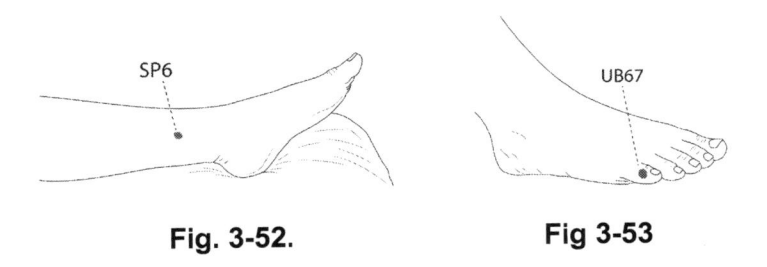

Fig. 3-52.   **Fig 3-53**

Spleen #6 - Acupuncture point (Fig.3-52)- a 4 finger (except the thumb) breadth from the top inner ankle bone beside the tibia. Urinary Bladder #67 - Acupuncture point (Fig. 3-53)

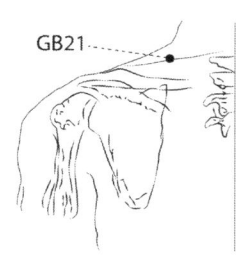

Fig. 3-54

Gall Bladder #21 point. (Fig.3-54) Midway between GV.14 point and the acromion at the high point of the shoulder. GV.14 -between the spinous processes of the 7th cervical vertebra and the first thoracic vertebra about the level of the shoulder.

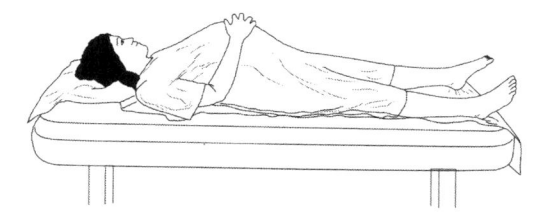

Fig. 3-55

Make circles 30 times with the two palms moving counterclockwise on your stomach - from your point of view. (Fig. 3-55)

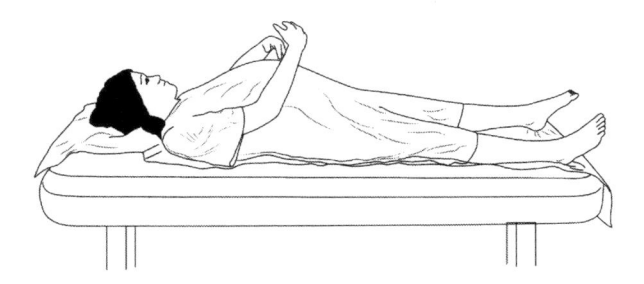

Fig. 3-56

Make counterclockwise circles 30 times while holding your two palms above your stomach without touching it. (Fig. 3-56)

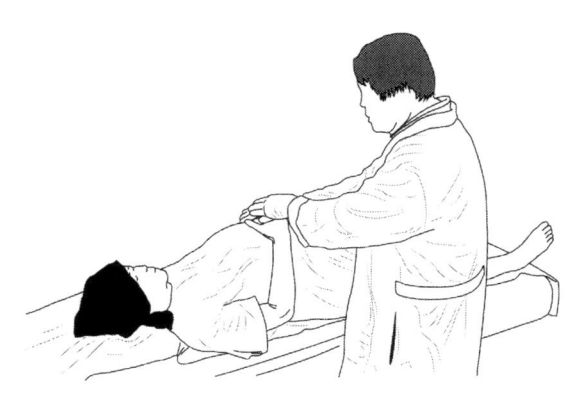

Fig. 3-57

Fig. 3-57: Make counterclockwise circles 30 times with two palms on your stomach with Doctor Kim.

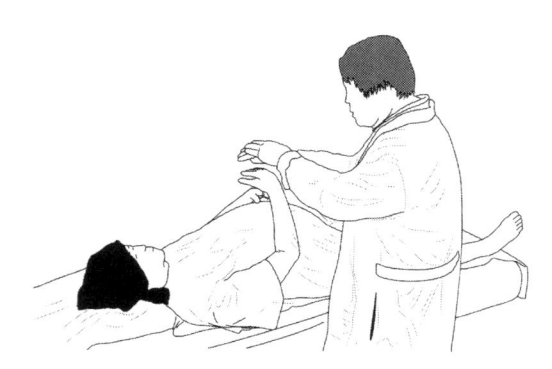

Fig. 3-58

Fig. 3-58: Make counterclockwise circles 30 times with two palms above your stomach without touching it with Doctor Kim. (Fig. 3-58)

If you feel that the baby's head is moving clockwise then you don't have to keep on turning your hands counterclockwise. Follow the direction baby's head is moving. If you are not sure of it then just keep on turning your hands counterclockwise.

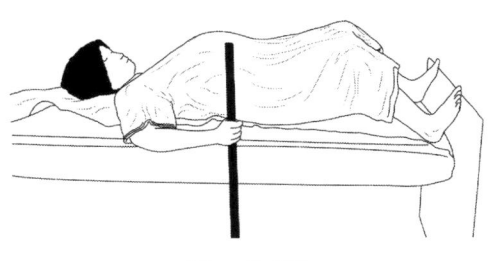

Fig. 3-59

Fig. 3-59 Lie down on your back, Pull the sticks with two hands and push bottom of the feet to the board for delivering the baby. (Fig.3-59)

Fig. 3-60

Lie down on your stomach, bend your knees. Push the sticks with two hands and push the bottoms of the feet to the board to deliver the baby. (Fig.3-60)

All hospitals should have this kind of bed. There are some beds with guard rails in nursing homes.

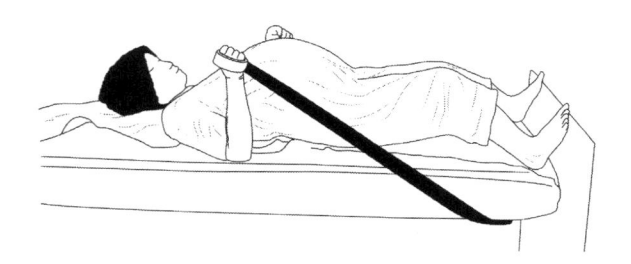

Fig. 3-61

Lie down on your back, Pull the belt with two hands and push bottom of the feet to the board to deliver the baby. (Fig.3-61)

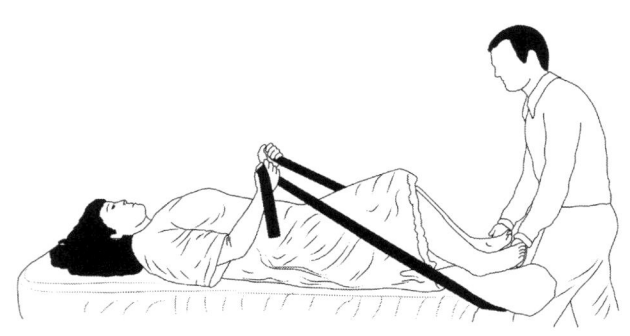

Fig. 3-62

Lie down on your back, Pull the belt with two hands and push bottom of the feet while husband hold the feet. (Fig.3-62)

Kneel down on the floor.

Fig.3-63

Push the walls or furniture with both hands at the same time push the wall with the bottoms of both feet. (Fig.3-63)

Fig.3-64

Then, kneel down on the floor, pushing the floor with both hands and feet like an animal delivering a baby. (Fig.3-64)

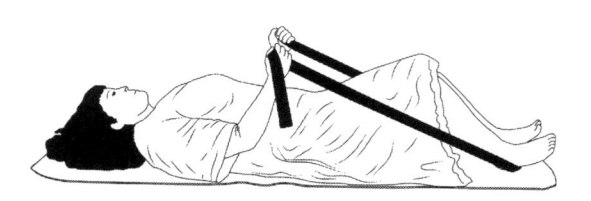

Fig.3-65

Lie down on the floor, pull the belt while pushing both feet against it. Both feet should be against the wall. (Fig.3-65)

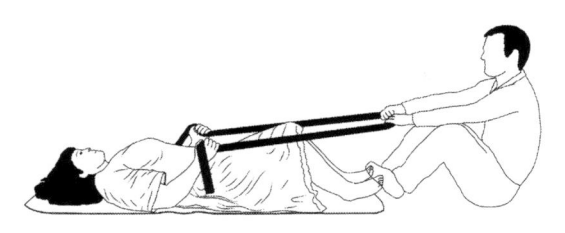

Fig.3-66

(Fig.3-66) Now, the wife and husband should pull the belt against each other and push with both feet against each other's feet.

A woman will have a greater chance of a Cesarean delivery if she has a back problem or had a previous C-section. This woman should receive acupuncture for her urinary bladder, her gall bladder and especially her Belt channel before becoming pregnant again. A woman with a very weak constitution or suffering from malnutrition through disease or diet should receive treatment for her spleen, stomach, kidney and heart channels. At the delivery table she should have a moxa treatment to these channels and points if the attending physician allows it. One should take caution while giving moxa treatments to a woman throughout her pregnancy **NOT** to treat these points: LI#4, SP#6, LiV#3, UB#40, UB#67 and GB#21. Treating these points could cause a miscarriage.

If a woman is treated during delivery at UB#67, on the side of her (lateral) small toenail with moxa for 30 minutes, it could prevent a breach delivery, as the baby's head will turn to its normal position. This method has a 90% success rate in China. During pregnancy, if the pregnant woman receives chi energy through acupuncture or through the palms without touch, if she receives this treatment once or twice a month until baby is delivered, then not only does the mother recover faster, but the baby is born with extra chi energy compared to other babies. The baby will be very healthy and energetic.

Stretching While Lying Down

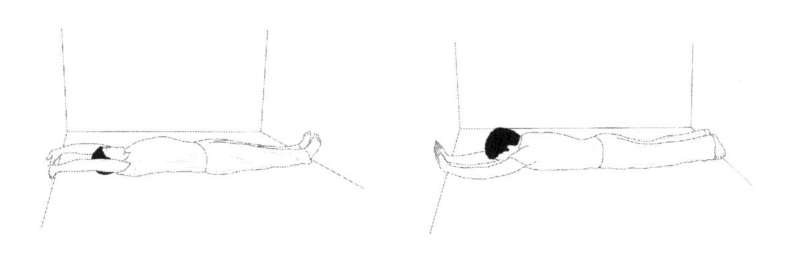

Fig. 3-67   **Fig. 3-68**

(Fig.3-67) Lie down on your back, stretch, and do the isometric exercise. First inhale through nose, and then exhale through the mouth doing 10 times per set and then end after pushing and exhale breathing. Hold your breath while pushing for 20 seconds - 5 times per a set.

(Fig.3-68) Lie down on your stomach and then push other hands and feet in both directions.

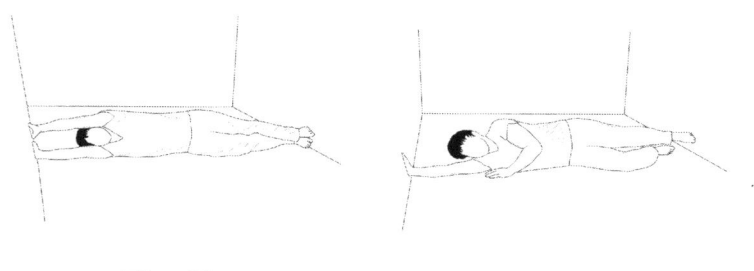

Fig. 69   **Fig. 70**

(Fig.3-69) Lie down on your side and push hands and feet to both directions.

(Fig. 3-70) Lie down on your side, fold the left arm and right leg and push hands and feet in both directions.

- Repeat this on the other side.

BOTTLES

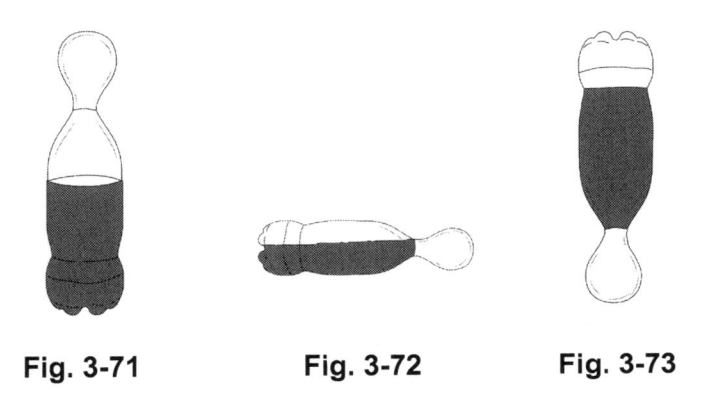

Fig. 3-71   **Fig. 3-72**   **Fig. 3-73**

(Fig. 3-71) **Bottle A** in Figure 3-71 shows the blood at 70% which is comparable to a man standing. This indicates that the process of blood circulating through the head and blood in the vein around the calf muscle is very difficult. Rub above the outer side ankle area with a small stick you will feel pain. Everyone has blood stagnation there. People with back, hip joint and/or hip pain will especially feel more pain on one side. Diabetic patients will especially have more pain. Remember to massage the area every day.

(Fig. 3-72) Bottle **B** in Figure 3-72 shows the blood field at 70% while kneeling like a four-legged animal. Blood circulating through the heart to the head and the blood in veins around calf muscle moving to the heart is much easier.

(Fig.3-73) **Bottle C** shows the blood field at 70 % like a man standing upside down - his blood circulating through the head and blood in the veins around the calf muscle moving to the heart is very smooth.

Fig. 3-74

(Fig.3-74) Lie on your back and raise both feet up against a wall.

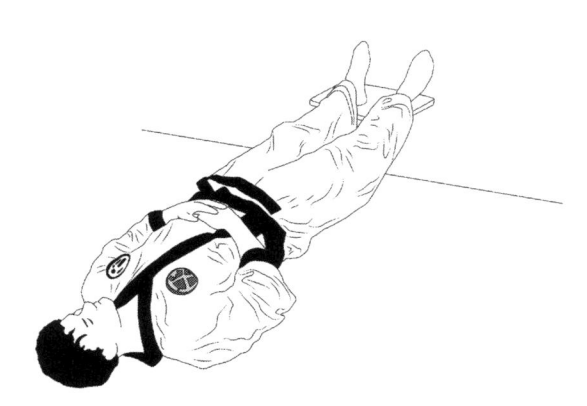

Fig. 3-75

(Fig.3-75) Lie on your back and raise both feet up against chair. People with high blood and/or eye pressure should do this movement.

Fig. 3-76
Fig. 3-76: Crawl like an infant by using palms and knees for older people

Fig. 3-77

Fig. 3-77: Bear crawl with palms and bottom of feet.

The Benefits of Crawling

Some anthropologists say Homo-Erectus was on this earth 1.8 million years ago and that due to gravitational forces pulling down on us, the skeletal structures of human beings have been changing since then. The human skull has gotten bigger due to brain development, the pelvic bones are smaller, and the cervical and neck vertebra are weak compared to our ancient ancestors.

The following information is commonly known amongst doctors of Oriental medicine. Our upper body has better blood circulation than the lower part of the body since our lower part has poor circulation due to the gravitational pressure from the upper body. Note the common occurrence of varicose veins in women.

When there is an injury in the hand or arm it heals faster than injuries to the leg. If one's foot is amputated, sometimes the infection does not heal, and the doctor cuts off more of the leg. This is not only true for diabetics, but healthy, young people, too. How can one prevent these problems?

A wise person crawls for at least ten minutes per day, with both palms and soles of the feet touching the ground. It will adjust alignment of the spine and will develop hands and feet, arms and legs, hips and shoulders, distributing weight proportionately. You can crawl on your palms and knees, but it is much less effective. Crawling stimulates internal organs.

Some exercises that work for balancing upper and lower parts of the body are swimming, yoga, Pilates, and crawling. Crawling is a good exercise as a warmup for limbering up before and after any sports activities. This is especially true for running.

What is the weakest part of our human body? It is the neck. One can simply watch a movie from the front row seat in a theater for an hour, or more, and get neck pain.

One will suffer much less with whiplash after a car accident if crawling every day has been implemented into the daily routine.

We have rehabilitation hospitals and medical research teams at research universities who would be wise to study the human benefits of Taoist style crawling. The research cannot be done properly with animals. Anyone who tries crawling for one week will get a good result. It's easy to prove.

Crawling is one of the martial artists' and Taoist's secrets of maintaining health and longevity. All athletes would be wiser to combine crawling with other training. In addition to breaking world records, crawling would enable athletes to keep their records longer. Even Olympians Michael Phelps and Usain Bolt should crawl!

A doctor of sports medicine said the 1970's were for running. The 1980's were the era of jogging and in the 1990's walking became vogue. I would like to add the 21st century is for Taoist crawling!

Head and neck

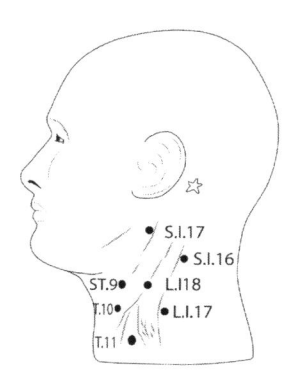

Fig. 3-78

Figure 3-78 is a side view of the head and neck. There are three Hand Yang Acupuncture channels with the hand end up there and three Yang of foot channels for Acupuncture starting there for governing and conception vessels. There are about one hundred and twenty acupuncture points in the head and neck excluding a hundred ear acupuncture points.

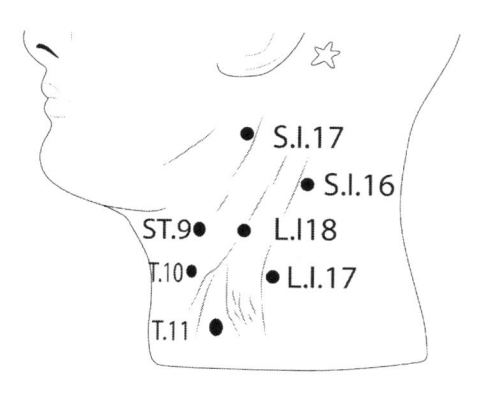

Fig. 3-79

Figure 3-79 is a close view of the neck with 2 points of the Small Intestine channel connected to the ear, 2 points of Large Intestine channel which are connected to the nose, and 3 points of the Stomach channel which are also connected to the eye. Also, the caved in area in the throat area is the Conceptional vessel #22 (in the center of the suprasternal fossa) and below the nose, a little above the midpoint of the philtrum, is the Governing vessel #26 for resuscitation. The neck area to the cheek has trigeminal nerves which are connected to the ear, eye, and mouth, too.

Why do we get wrinkles, thyroid problems, Alzheimer's, Parkinson's, ear, eye, throat and mouth problems as we get older?

Compare humans to animals. We have poor blood circulation through our lifetime. So, you must do the above exercises and an all ten fingers massage to the entire head, around the eyes, mouth and press and also, pinch the sternocleidomastoid muscle around neck. Hold the ear and wiggle it few times.

One case history is of a 45-year-old woman college professor who complained of Hashimoto-Hypothyroid problems. I showed her how to crawl, raise her feet up, head and neck massage, and once per week acupuncture treatment for two weeks, When she visited me on the third week, her endocrine specialist told her that her TSH level had changed from 7 down to 2. It was now within a normal range.

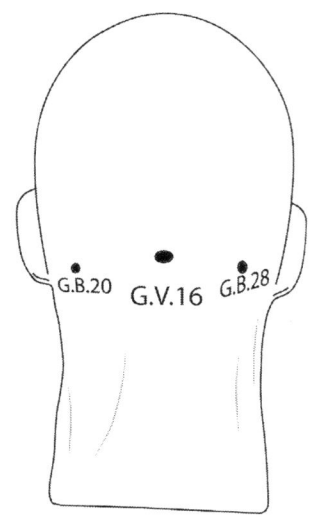

Fig. 3-80

There are three Wind Points of Acupuncture in the back of the neck area just below the occipital bone. It is believed that cold wind goes through these points and people get cold. So, you must wear a scarf or muffler during the winter season to cover this area.

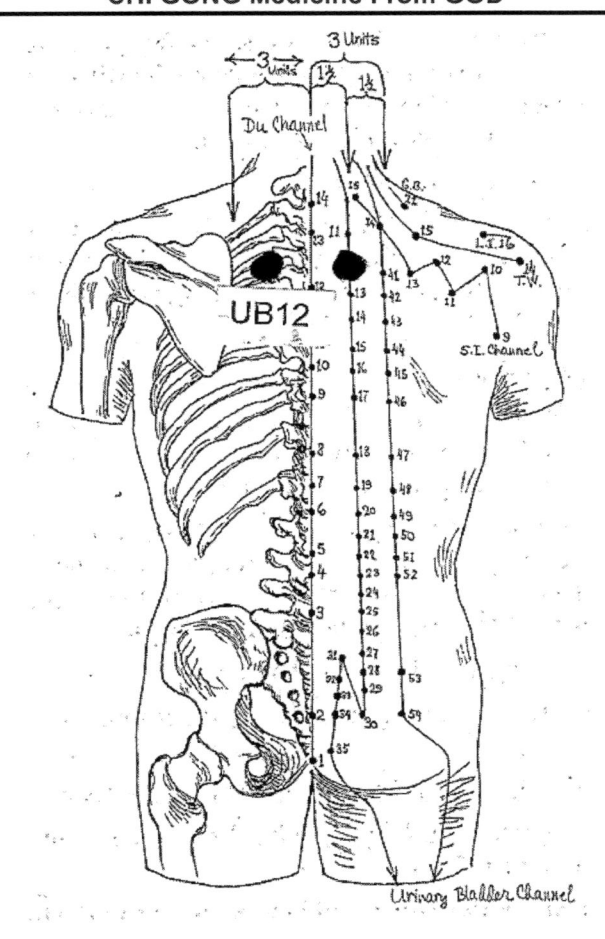

Fig. 3-81

GV. 16 Feng Fu- Wind House – Directly below the occipital protuberance in the depression.

UB. 12 Feng Men-Wind Gate – Mid way between the 2nd thoracic vertebra and the medial edge of the scapula.

GB.20 Feng Chi-Wind Lake - Below the occipital bone in the depression between the upper portion of the M. Sternocleidomastoid and M. Trapezius.

Developing Sexual Energy and Techniques with Chi Gong

By practicing Chi Gong breathing exercises, one builds up chi energy at the navel area. In the case of women, this will stimulate the ovaries, and in the case of men, the prostate gland. With more sex hormones being generated, one is better able to use the Taoist Chi Gong method of sexual technique, which relies on anal contraction. This method is one of the best for developing the contraction of vaginal muscles, and also helps treat premature ejaculation.

Chi Gong, Yoga or Dr. - Kegel Exercise

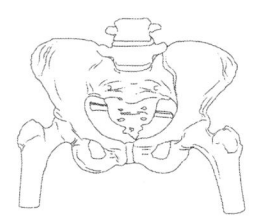

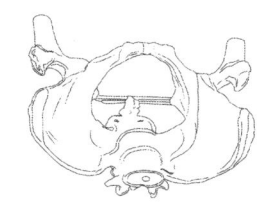

Fig. 3-82   Fig. 3-83

(Fig. 3-82) Is the front view of the hip bone - There is an anus, penis, prostate, urethra and urinary bladder for a man and a vagina, uterus, ovary, anus, urethra, and urinary bladder for a woman. Running, jogging, walking and weightlifting do not much stimulate muscles of the above listed organs. Yoga, Chi gong and Kegel exercises will strengthen the muscles properly and prevent many diseases with these organs. These exercises will facilitate sexual functions for both sexes. Other benefits are numerous. For example, woman experience urine leaking while coughing or laughing sometime around 50 years of age, or so. The Kegel exercise is the solution. Fig.3-83 is the back view of the hip bone.

Fig. 3-84

Fig. 3-84 First, inhale and exhale but leave a little air and squeeze the anus muscle lightly for 5 seconds and then exhale through the mouth for 5 seconds.

Fig. 3-85

Fig. 3-85 Do this exercise the same as above, but this time hold and squeeze a small soft ball in each hand while squeezing the anus muscle. It makes this exercise less boring and grabbing power is one of indication of body health for senior citizens.

In this technique, a man should try to breathe longer during sex, counting slowly forward or backward as he inhales and exhales. Just before ejaculation he should hold his breath and by contracting his anus like squeezing a ball to pull chi energy toward his body and away from the penis. One can then press point Ren 1 between the anus and scrotum with a finger or cotton swab, not too hard or too soft, in order to control ejaculation. This technique takes a great deal of practice and experience. A person with an enlarged or cancerous prostate should not attempt this technique.

If both the man and woman have advanced experience with breathing exercises and an abundance of chi energy, they can exchange chi energy during sex. This is an ideal form if yin/yang exchange and harmony, and both partners will actually feel more energized. This procedure also takes many years of practice.

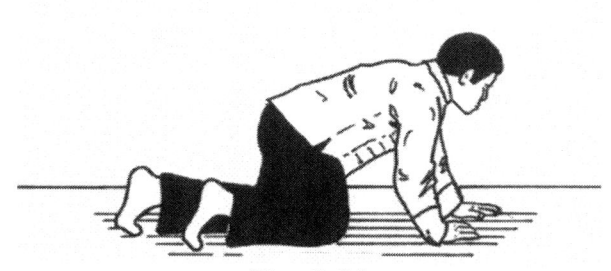

Fig. 3-86

The four-legged crawl position (Fig. 3-86) is beneficial for many reasons. First, it helps us humans recover a muscle balance between our upper and lower bodies. We notice that four-legged animals have an equally distributed use of all four limbs when walking while we humans walk on just two feet.

Our walking naturally leads to a weakness of development in our neck and shoulders, especially if we do no lifting or strenuous upper body exercise during the day. Our standing upright also means that gravity pulls our upper body downwards, putting extra stress on hips and legs to bear this weight. Now, think about the tiger. It carries its cubs around. It attacks a 500-pound cow and picks it up with its jaws; it drags its prey for miles and miles across land; it even swims across a river with it. This shows amazing neck and shoulder strength. The sled dogs used by Eskimos are the same way. Their necks and shoulders handle a tremendous amount of stress. The four-legged crawl position can alleviate some of our own imbalanced development, relieving back pain and strengthening the lumbar region in the process.

In our modern age, we notice that younger women have a hard time recuperating from childbirth when compared to women in previous generations. Their grandmothers or great grandmothers, especially if they engaged in heavy physical labor (e.g., farming), were able to have children and bounce back very quickly. The four-legged crawl is one way to correct for the lack of exercise that working at a desk in these modern times produces. This crawl is especially important for elderly people, since it helps to distribute weight to all joints (instead of just knees, hips, and ankles) while strengthening the neck and shoulders. Younger people who want to increase sexual energy should do this exercise every day.

Crawling is a very important exercise for rehabilitation after such injuries as stroke or surgery because it exercises many groups of muscles in a balanced way, as does swimming, but without the risk of drowning or even of falling since one is already down on all fours.

Fig. 3-87

We see that in the crawl position both palms are touching the ground, receiving chi energy from the earth (yin energy). Fig. 3-87 is a slightly different variation, in which one puts pillows or other soft support under the ankles. In this position we see that the palms receive chi from the earth and the feet, now elevated and pointed upwards, receive chi from the sky. This yin/yang balance is the opposite of that of the standing position, where the feet touch the ground, and the palms face upwards.

From this position (Fig. 3-87), inhale slowly, hold the breath, and exhale slowly. Every third time you hold your breath, contract the anus muscle before exhaling. There are two different ways to circulate chi in this position, as described in the Taoist Chi Gong section. Practice both methods.

Fig. 3-88

In Fig. 3-88 we see that both the palms and the soles of the feet are facing the ground, as in a modified "push-up" pose. Thus, both hands and feet receive yin energy chi from the earth. As with Fig. 3-87 practice both types of chi circulation in this position. (Note: Fig. 3-87 will be preferable for older people and those with less low and upper body strength, whereas Fig. 3-88 might be easier for young people.)

Fig. 3-89

The opposite of this yin energy position is Fig.3-89, where the palms and the soles of the feet face upwards. This of course allows one to receive chi energy from the heavens, which is yang energy. Again, practice the Taoist type Chi Gong breathing exercises in this position.

How to Prevent Altitude Sickness and the "Bends" or Deep-Sea Diver's Sickness

High altitude

At 14,000 feet (4,000 meters) the air contains about 60% of the oxygen that is present at sea level. Everyone, from vacationers to the most seasoned of mountain climbers, will experience altitude sickness at this level; many will experience it at much lower levels such as 6,500 feet (1,400 meters). While the severity will vary based on each individual, the symptoms of altitude sickness are the same: headache, nausea/vomiting, sleep disturbance and rapid heartbeat.

At lower levels, one or two days at rest will improve your condition. Expeditions to Mt. Everest – 28,000 feet above sea level – require 5-6 weeks of acclimatization to get the body used to the level of oxygen present in the air.

High altitude pulmonary edema

If you ascend too rapidly, 10,000 feet (3,000 meters) within 2-3 days, or fly into an area of this height, you can develop dyspnea, or fluid in the lungs. The symptoms include coughing up white or bloody phlegm and a rapid heartbeat or coughing and chest conditions similar to pneumonia. If this occurs, you must return to low altitude levels immediately. If this condition is present in the brain, you may get hemorrhage and die.

If you get altitude sickness, the following herbal formula can help restore lung functions.

Herbal Prescription for High Altitude Edema

Huang Qi, Radix Astragali -Yellow Vetch Root.......15 grams
Fu Ling, Poria Cocaos -Hoelen...........................9 grams
Xing Ren, Semem Armeniacae Amarae - Apricot Seed
......9 grams
Tao Ren, Semen Persicae - Peach Seed.............9 grams
Gan Cao, Radix Glycyrrihizae - Licorice Root.........6 grams
Chen Pi, Pericarpium Citri Reticulatae – Tangerine Peel
.......9 grams
Ban Xia, Rhizoma Pinelliae - Pinelliae Root ....9 grams
Gan Jang, Rhizoma Zingiberis - Dried Ginger.........9 grams

Use the above as a standard formula and add more herbs for each individual's need according to the diagnosis and evaluation by a Doctor of Oriental Medicine. You can grind it up to make a pill.

Acupuncture is best for restoring lung functions, and you should also massage or apply moxa to the lung channels.

But there are precautions you can take before you go to high altitude that can prevent or lessen the severity of the symptoms, including Chi Gong breathing. Any kind of Chi Gong breathing exercise is beneficial for altitude sickness, but Buddhist style is best – because in the Buddhist style, you inhale and exhale longer than your normal breathing pattern, allowing you to exhale more carbon dioxide than you would in normal breathing while keeping more oxygen in your body. Unlike normal breathing, you do not lose a lot of oxygen when you exhale.

If you have not previously practiced Chi Gong and are going climbing, you should climb about 1,000 feet (300 meters) per day and practice Chi Gong breathing for 30 minutes - 1 hour, 2 times each day. When you reach 20,000 feet (6,000 meters) your red blood cell count may increase to compensate for the lack of oxygen. But this will be temporary.

It is important to note that people who live in high altitudes, such as in Tibet or in the Andes, have a high red blood cell count, and may experience high blood pressure problems if they move closer to sea level. Perhaps more importantly, if people move from high altitude to low or vice versa, and Chi Gong breathing does not help, they should return to the altitude of their origin.

Diving

Diving to great depths and even shallow water diving at seven feet can cause a problem, because as Boyle's law states, the volume of a given mass of gas varies inversely with the pressure exerted upon it. Whether a diver holds his/her breath or uses an oxygen tank, the deeper the water is, the greater the pressure and the higher density of air in the lungs. This can cause an over-flow of gas molecules – O_2, CO_2, and N – and in the case of O_2 or CO_2 leads to toxicity, or nitrogen narcosis, which resembles alcohol intoxication. When a diver ascends, this causes gas embolism in pulmonary arteries or cerebral arteries resulting in loss of consciousness or death.

When Ninja or military special forces in Asia dive, they typically hold the root of a plant in one hand and a cut stem of the plant in the other hand, which they put in their mouth to use as a snorkel. This is because the stems of most aquatic plants are hollow, like a hose, to carry air.

The following is one type of Taoist breathing method for divers:

Inhale through nose	Hold	Exhale through nose	Hold
5 seconds	15 secs.	4 secs.	3 secs.

or in a pattern of the same ratio

You can see that this method is different than most other forms of Chi Gong breathing as you hold your breath even after you exhale. When you inhale and exhale through your nose, you must have your breath be as thin as a thread. Over the course of time, you should hold your breath longer with each practice. With this ratio of breath, if you can achieve a total of 3 minutes. It is a small success!

Hypothermia

Whether you travel to high altitudes or dive down into the deep sea, your body temperature will decrease. To warm up, first rub your hands and feet for a few minutes. Then assume the pose in Figure 3-8. Refer to page 76, "How to Lose Weight". Use this internal breathing technique on page 76 and hold your breath longer but this time, move the air up and down and up and down and up and down inside your stomach before breathing out and exhaling with shhhhh and poo poo poo sound. As you advance, your body can get hotter and you can try this even ten times a day. You can use this even in cold weather in the Arctic Circle.

Moxa/Moxibustion

Moxibustion is a method for treating and preventing diseases through the application of heat to certain acupuncture points. Moxa is usually found in the shape of a cigar and is made of mugwort leaves (Folium Artemisia Argyi).

As mentioned earlier, acupuncture is very effective when curing acute problems. Moxa generates a great deal of heat, and when applied near or on the skin surface, helps to relieve channel obstructions caused by dampness or cold. Moxibustion is effective in curing chronic problems such as stomach problems or indigestion, coldness, numbness and weakness. Moxa is a tonification method which can be used by everyone.

After moxibustion, the white and red corpuscles and the body's immunity to disease are increased. The revival ability of cellular tissue is improved as after an injection of protein.

Blood circulation, absorption of nutrition, bodily function and metabolism are improved as is the skeletal strength.

The ways to apply moxa include through a moxa cone, moxa stick, or on the head of an acupuncture needle. It can be applied either directly or indirectly. In the case of a moxa cone, lit moxa is placed directly on the skin. Depending on the nature of the disease, the moxa can be left on the skin to cause a burn or can be removed and replaced with another cone if the first one gets too hot (Figure 3-90).

To apply a moxa cone indirectly, the doctor will cover the point with a slice of ginger, garlic or salt. A moxa stick is applied by bringing the lit moxa close to the skin then moving it away (Figure 3-91). Placing a lit piece of moxa on an acupuncture needle is the third method of application (Figure 3-92)

How to Apply Moxa Stick

When purchasing moxa, I recommend the smokeless type which is made of mugwort leaves (Folium Artemisiae Argyi). This is usually ¼ inch diameter and 4½ inches long. First, wrap the stick with aluminum foil to prevent an unwanted smell on your fingers. Second, light the moxa stick with a cigarette lighter, or the flame on a stove. It will take a few minutes before the moxa starts to burn. Third, warm the acupuncture point or asi[25] points. To keep from accidentally burning yourself, use your edge of the palm as a guide by placing it near the spot you are treating (see Figure 3-91).

Place the burning moxa about ½ inch from the skin above the acupuncture point. Do not hold it stationary, move the moxa around a circle of 1 inch diameter. Do this for a few seconds until the skin starts to feel hot then move to another point. Make sure you tap the stick to shake-off loose ashes to prevent accidental burning.

Treat yourself with moxa for about 15 minutes on both the front and back of your body. If your condition is acute or chronic and time allows, apply moxa two or three times a day. In an emergency such as severe indigestion or a heart attack, use warm water on the hands and feet first and then apply moxa to the hands and feet. Then treat the front points around the abdomen. After treatment, extinguish the moxa fire with water and let dry for a few days.

Use another moxa stick alternately. You do not need to know exactly where the acupuncture point is. Moxa anywhere near the points will be effective in moving Chi and blood stagnation in your body.

Figures for Moxa Treatment

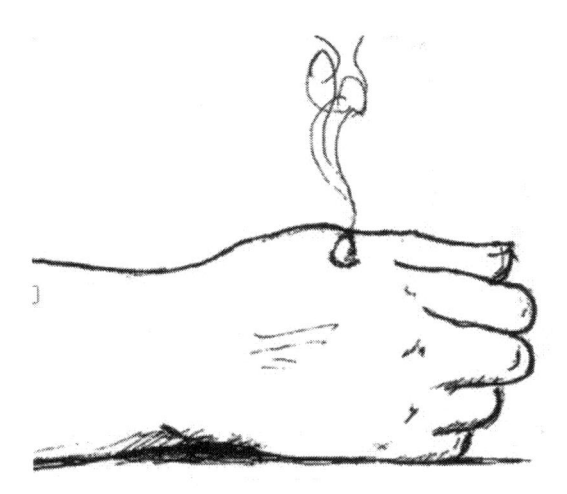

Fig. 3-90

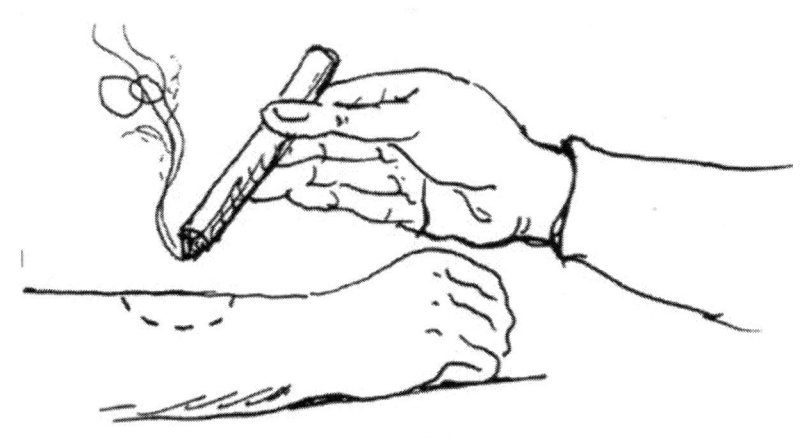

Fig. 3-91

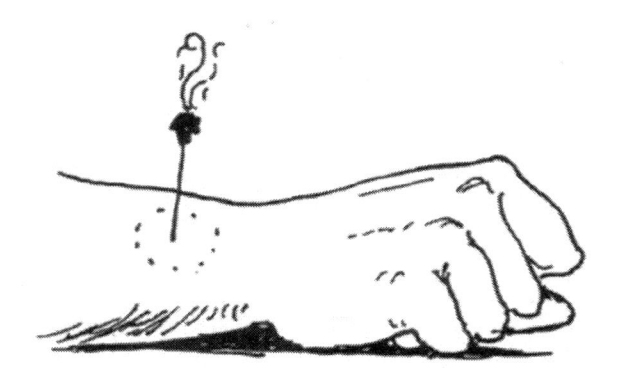

Fig. 3-92

Moxa Treatment and Chi Gong

Moxa treatment is a form of chi-tonifying method and is beneficial for most people and is especially good for Chi Gong practitioners. One should receive a diagnosis and evaluation from a licensed acupuncturist to learn which channels and points have Chi stagnation and locations of points. Buddhist priests have moxa treating ceremonies during the fall season at some temples in Japan. They usually put burning moxa cones on each other's shoulders and at other few points. It is a good method against catching a cold or flu during the cold winter season. Most of the acupuncture points are located between muscles, and if pressed forcefully with the fingertips, will cause pain or paralysis for short periods of time. Some of the points may be very sensitive and could cause pain because there is chi stagnation at that point. Sometimes you can find a point that is very painful to touch other than an acupuncture point. It is called an Asi point.[25] You should treat that point as well. You should not do moxa treatment when you have a high fever. Also, you should not do moxa on ulcerated skin surface or an infected area. It is good for areas with a skin rash.

Proportional Measurements

Unit: A unit of measurement used to locate points. The length of one unit depends upon the body shape of the individual patient as well as the part of the body being measured. One unit of the arm and one unit of the leg will be different in one person. Also, a child and an adult will be different. Between two nipples is measured as 8 units.

The lateral side of the thigh, the distance from the prominence of the greater trochanter to the middle of patella is 19 units. **The medial aspect of the leg**, the distance from the lower border of the medial condyle of the tibia to the tip of medial malleolus is 13 units. **The lateral side of the leg**, the distance between the center of the patella and the tip of the lateral malleolus is 16 units.

Look on the internet for acupuncture points.

Locations of Acupuncture Points

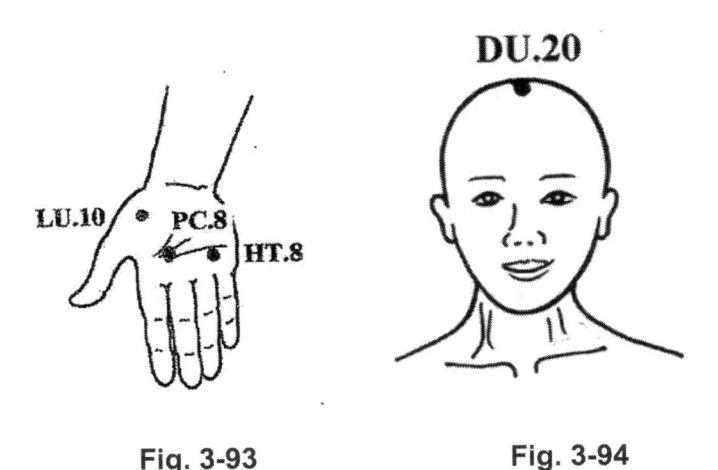

Fig. 3-93

Fig. 3-94

Locations of Acupuncture Points

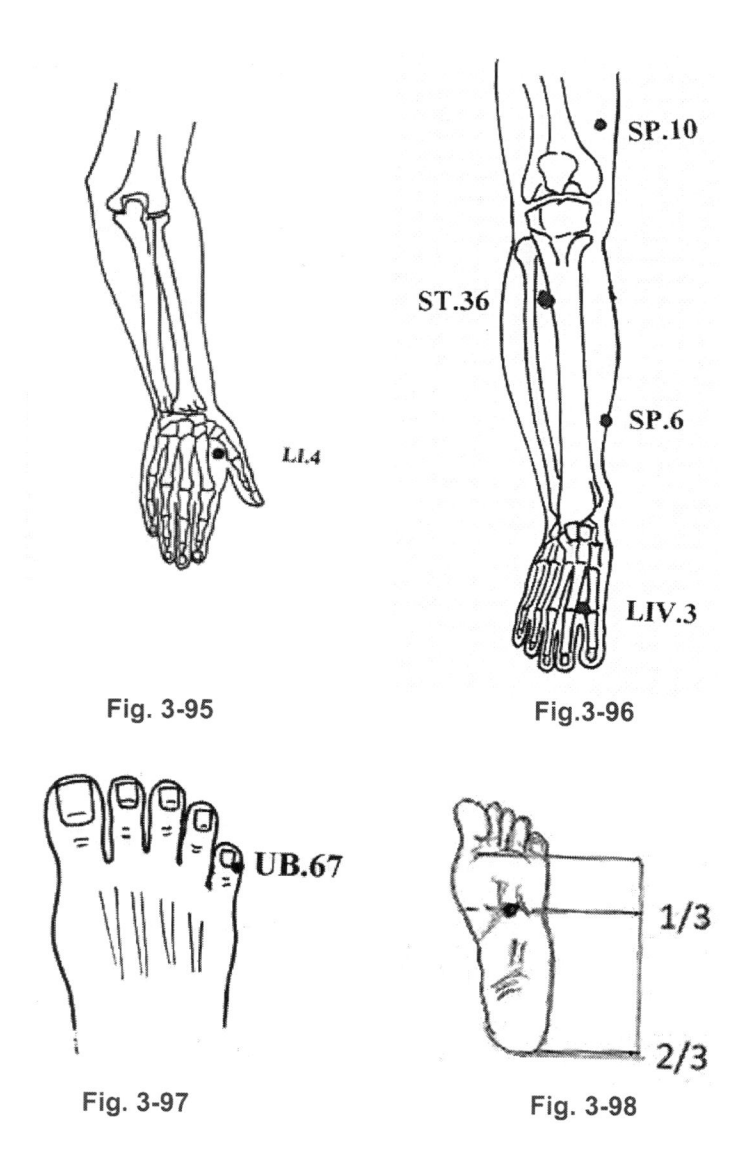

Fig. 3-95

Fig. 3-96

Fig. 3-97

Fig. 3-98

Lung #10 - On the radial side of the midpoint of the first metacarpal bone, on the junction of the red and white skin. (Fig. 3-93)

Heart #8 - On the palmar surface, between the fourth and the fifth metacarpal bones. If you make a fist, the point will be where the tip of the little finger rests. (Fig. 3-93)

Pericardium #8 - Between the second and third metacarpal bones, when you look at your palm. It is proximal to the metacarpophalangeal joint. (Fig. 3-93)

Du #20 - On the top of the head, on the midpoint of the line connecting the top of both ears. (Fig. 3-94)

Large Intestine #4 - Between the first and second metacarpal bones. This point is very sensitive to finger pressure. (Fig. 3-95)

Liver #3 - In the depression distal to the junction of the first and second metatarsal bones. This point is very sensitive to finger pressure. (Fig. 3-96)

Stomach #36 - 3 units below the side of the patella tip. One finger-width from the anterior crest of the tibia. (Fig. 3-96)

Spleen #6 - 3 units directly above the tip of the medial malleolus, on the posterior border of the tibia. (Fig. 3-96)

Spleen #10 - Flex your knee joint; it is 2 units above the medial superior border of the patella on the bulge of the medial portion of quadriceps femoris. (Fig. 3-96)

Urinary Bladder #40 - On the midpoint of the crease that is located at the back side of the knee between the tendons of biceps muscle femoris and semitendinosus muscle. (Fig. 3-99)

Urinary Bladder #60 - In the depression between the external malleolus and tendon calcaneus. (Fig. 3-98)

Urinary Bladder #67 - On the lateral side of the small toe, about 2mm posterior to the corner of the nail. (Fig. 3-97)

Liver #8 - On the medial side of the knee joint. (Fig. 3-100)

Liver #9 - 4 units above the medial epicondyle of the femur, between the vastus medialis muscle and the sartorius muscle. (Fig. 3-100)

Liver #10 - 3 units below the stomach 30. (Fig. 3-100)

Liver #11 - 2 units below stomach 30, on the lateral border of abductor longus muscle. (Fig. 3-100)

Stomach #30 - 5 units below the naval, 2 units lateral to Ren #2, superior to the inguinal groove on the medial side of the femoral artery. (Fig. 3-102)

Gall Bladder #30 - At the junction of the middle and lateral third of the distance between the greater trochanter and the hiatus of the sacrum. (Fig. 3-101, 3-109, 3-110)

Gall Bladder #31 - On the midline of the lateral side of the thigh, 7 units above the transverse popliteal crease. (Fig. 3-101, 3-107)

Gall Bladder #40 - On the anterior and inferior to the external malleolus, in depression on the lateral side of the tendon of extensor digitorum longus muscle. (Fig. 3-101)

Tan Tien (Ren#6 - On the midline of the abdomen 1.5 units below the naval. The distance between the naval and the upper border of symphysis pubis is 5 units. (Fig 3-102)

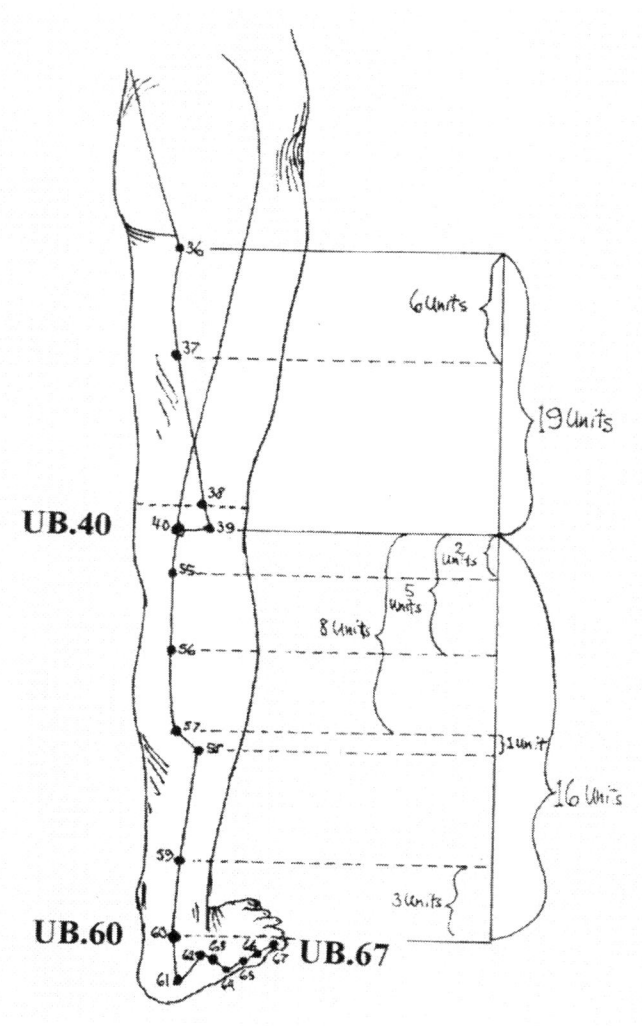

Fig. 3-99

Leg Urinary Bladder Channel

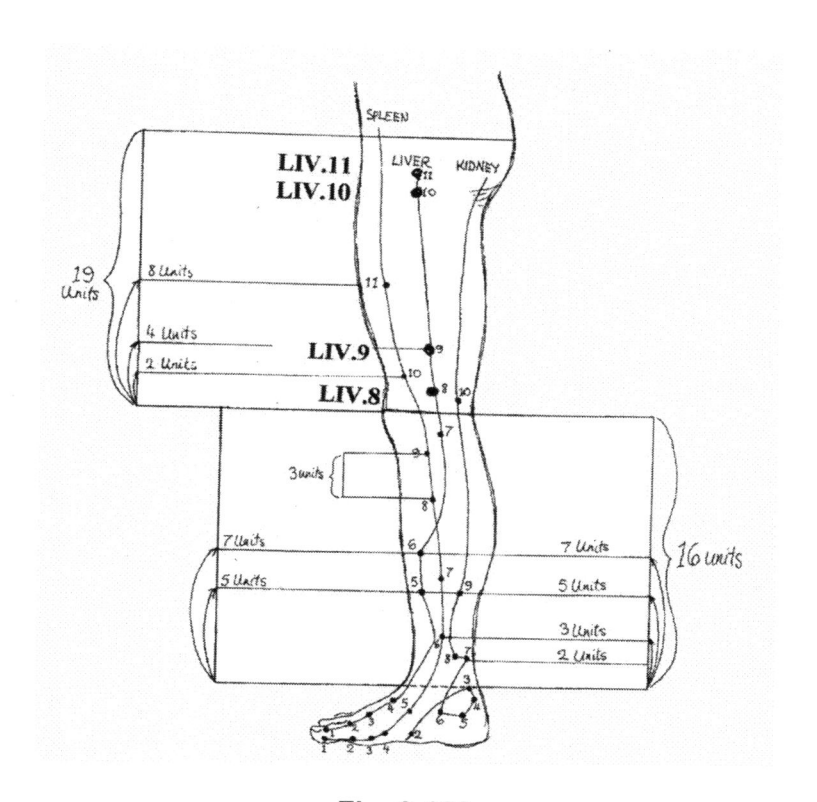

Fig. 3-100

Leg Yin Channel

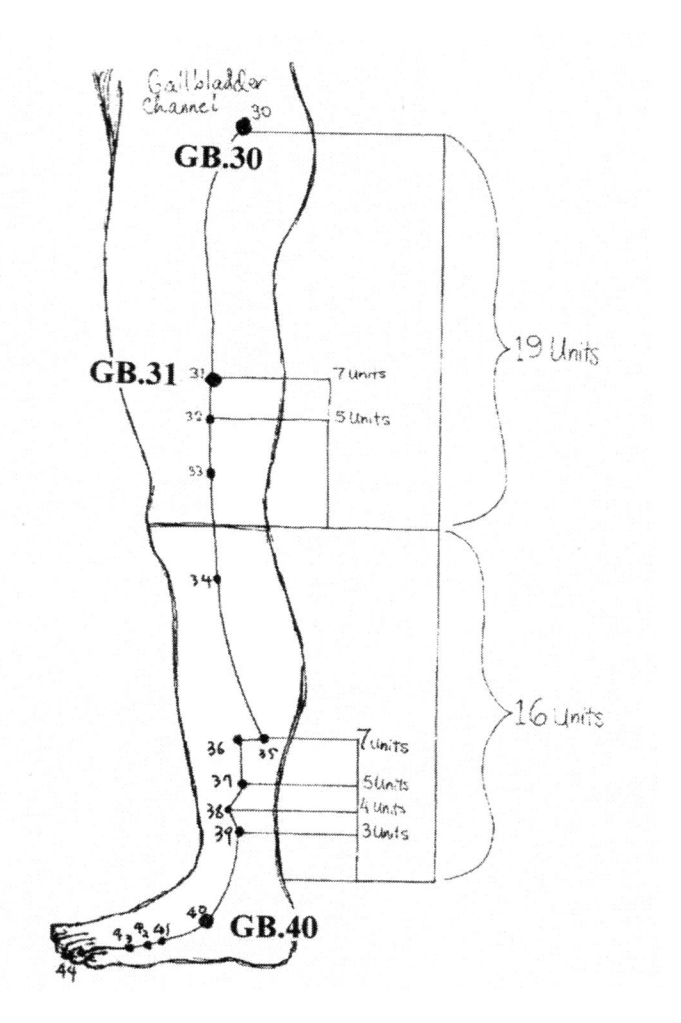

Fig. 3-101

Leg Gall Bladder Channel

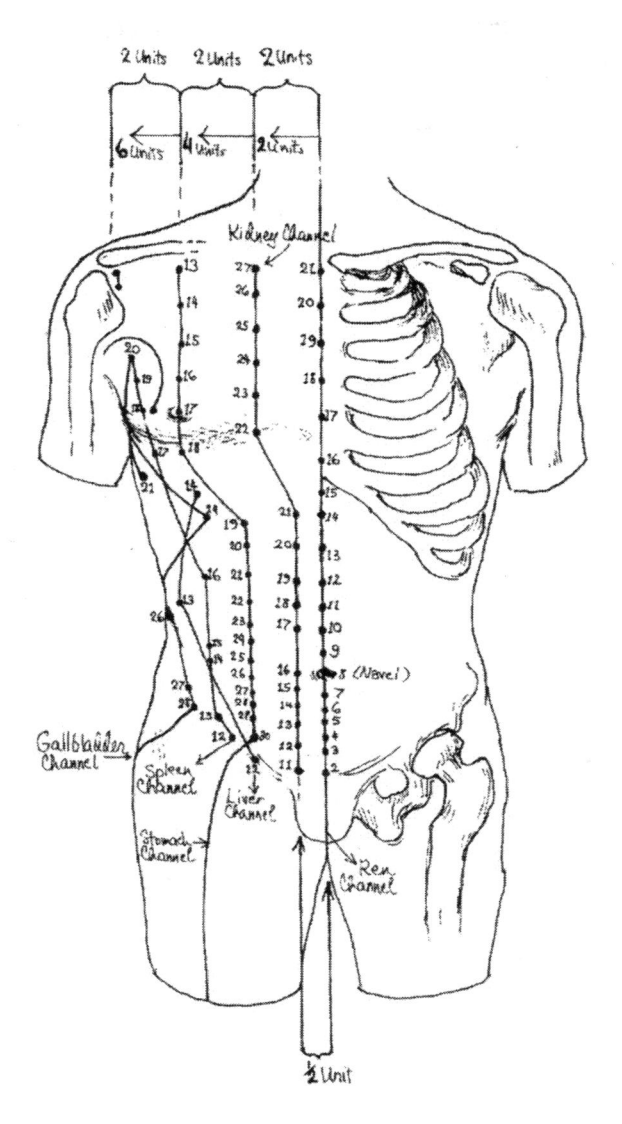

Fig. 3-102

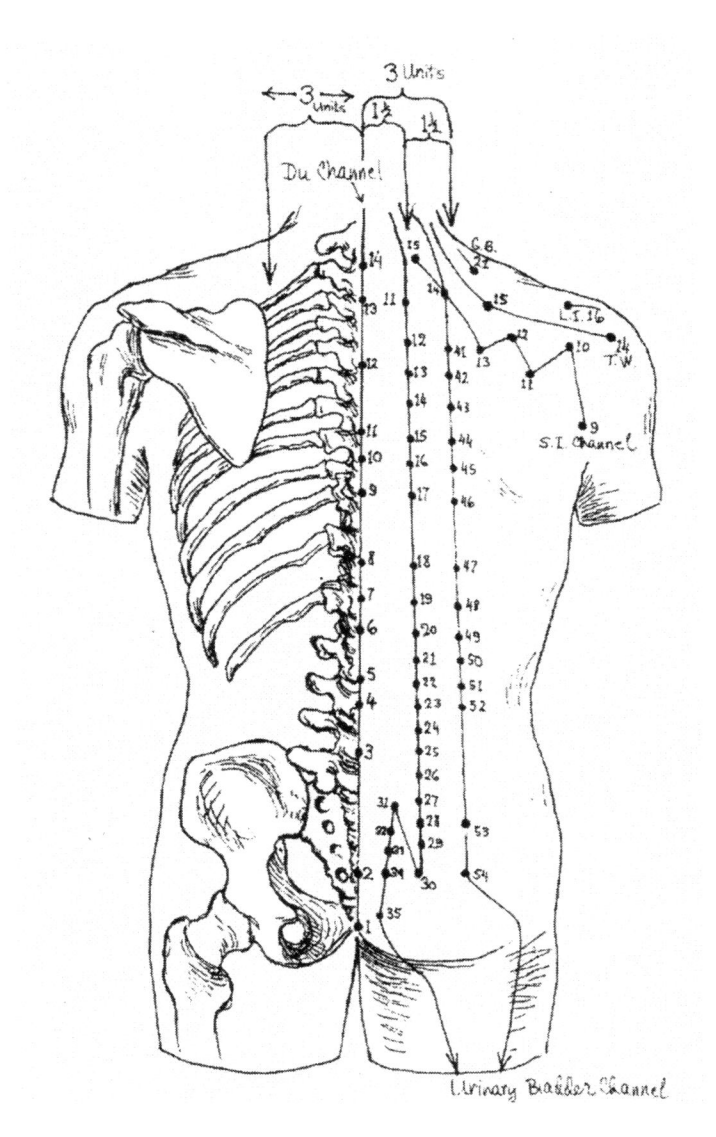

Fig. 3-103

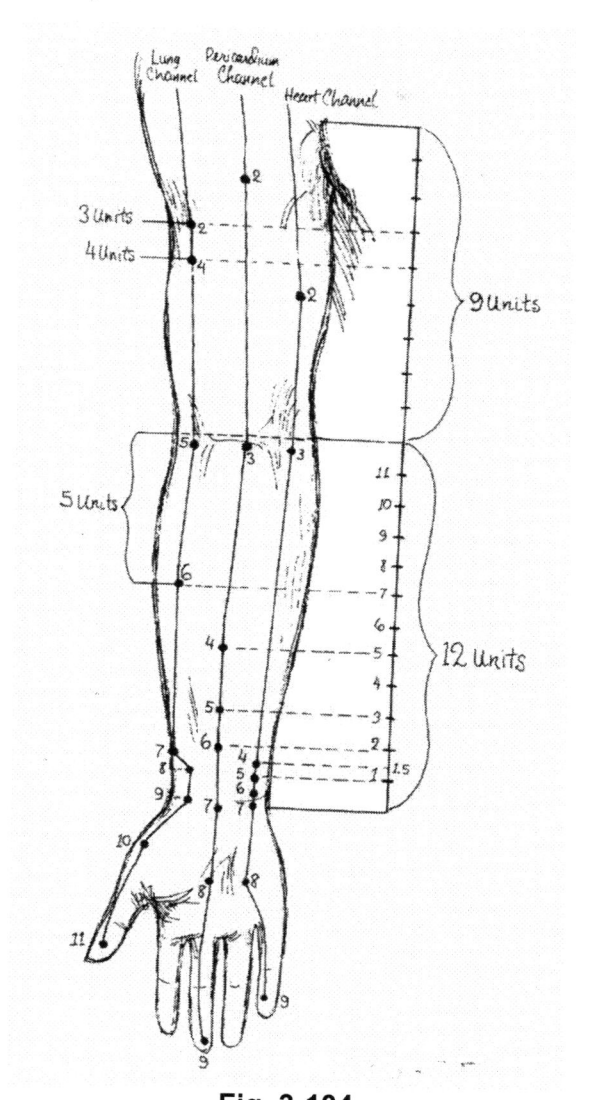

Fig. 3-104
Arm Yin Channels

132   Learning and Practicing Chi Gong

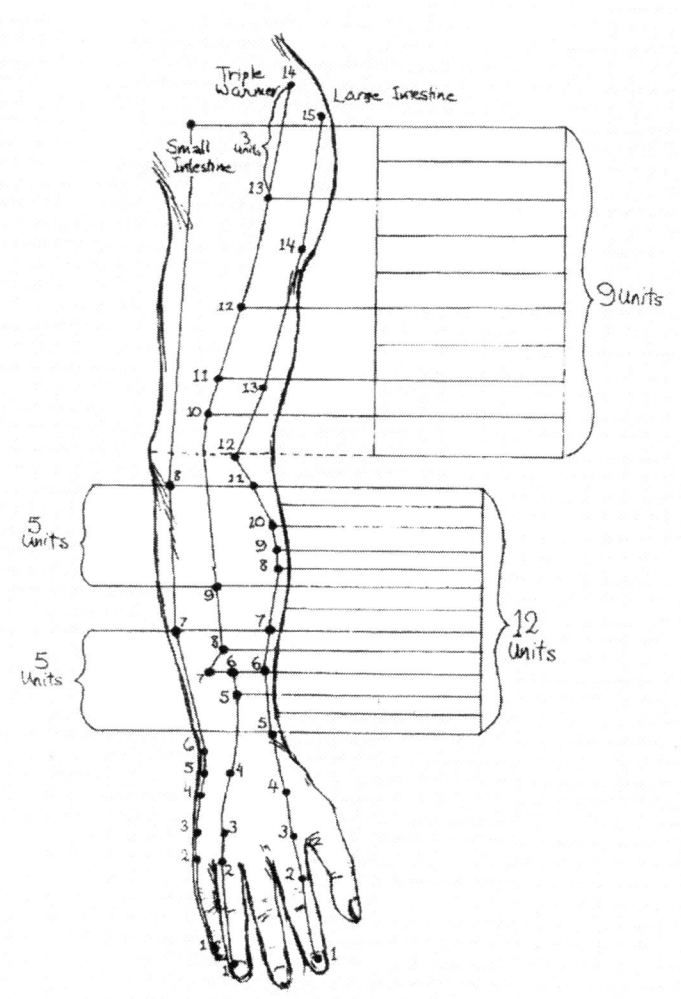

Fig. 3-105

Arm Yang Channels

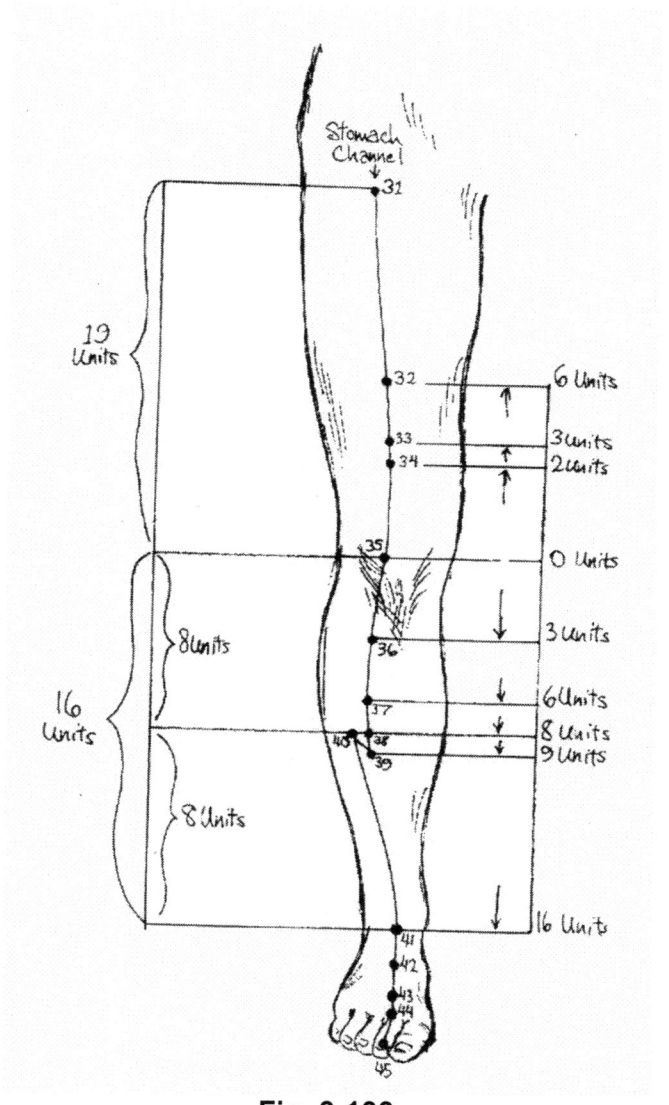

Fig. 3-106

Leg Stomach Channels

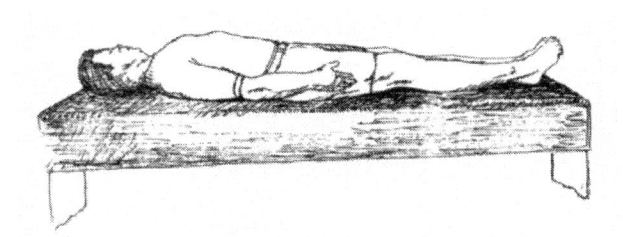

Fig. 3-107

Lie down on your back. In this position, you can check GB#31 by pressing with the tip of your middle finger while you hold your arms in the "attention" position.

Fig. 3-108

First bend your knees up so that the soles of your feet are flat on the floor. This will relax your abdominal muscles, allowing you to check GB#28. This point is just above and inside your hip bone (anterior superior iliac spine), for possible hernia, tilted uterus, or even ovary/uterine prolapse problems.

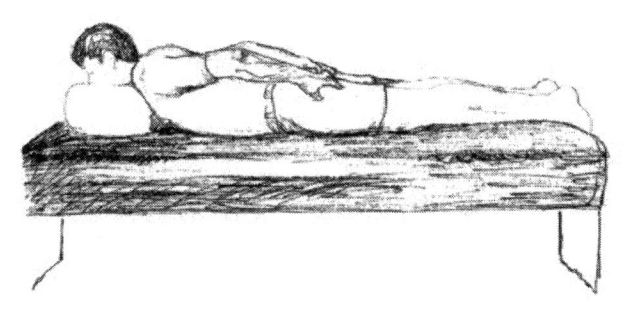

Fig. 3-109

First you should turn over onto your stomach. In this position, you can check GB#30, located on your hip. If lying on your stomach causes discomfort, you can lie on your side and press on GB#30 (see Fig. 3-110). Extend your small finger to the side and place it on your anus. Next fold up your three middle fingers as if you were making a fist. Extend the thumb towards the hip (near the great trochanter bone).

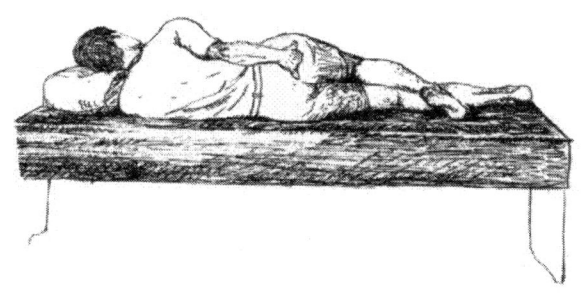

Fig. 3-110

CHAPTER 4
Experiences While Practicing Chi Gong

When we practice external styles such as Olympic sports and martial arts – Tae Kwon Do, Karate, Judo – we have the same type of experiences, including muscle soreness, weight loss, and increase in appetite. But when we practice Chi Gong, even after the first lesson, each person's experiences are different.

A woman may experience more spiritual phenomena than a man as women are typically more psychic in nature. Older men or even younger men with a large muscle mass, such as weight lifters, those with surgical scars or physical injuries (spinal at the neck and back) will need to practice a longer period of time to feel chi flow. Sometimes it could take months. (See the section entitled "Caution" for more details.)

If one practices Chi Gong in the wrong fashion, one will experience a constant physical pain, headache, depression, anger, sadness, tiredness, hyperactivity, insomnia or show signs of possession by an evil spirit. Usually, when one practices Chi Gong correctly, one will become calmer, have good digestion, have normal menstruation cycles, feel an increase in chi energy, feel lighter while walking, and be able to walk an increased distance without feeling tired. If you practice Chi Gong at least one hour per day, six months later your skin will have become clearer and have a luster, your eyes will be more clear and shinier, and your lips will become redder. Even if you take in small amounts of food, you will not feel hungry, and you can think more clearly. A student's academic effort will be much improved, and business people will get new ideas and have increased stamina. A few young people may levitate one or several feet off the ground for 5-30 minutes. This can happen during sleep or during the day while sitting on the floor in a Buddhist Chi Gong pose. It can happen one or two times during your lifetime. It can happen more if you can control it voluntarily as Jesus when he walked on water, Moses, Buddha, yogis, and a few Taoist masters have done throughout history.

An abundance of chi energy can help you survive an accident, as long as there are no severe cuts or heavy bleeding. In much the same way that a person who is drunk falls from a high building and survives, Chi Gong practitioners can survive. They do this by inhaling and exhaling, or by yelling, rather than the ordinary person who gets scared and stops breathing, therefore tightening their body and bones.

The Chi Gong practitioner knows that breathing and/or yelling will envelop and seal the body with chi. There are additional physical and mental strengths that help them survive as well. Some have been developed into instinctive habits, whether they realize this or not.

Sometimes a woman dreams in color, and the colors are so vivid compared to ordinary dreams she realizes that these previous images were black and white or unclear colors. Sometimes a color picture or image appears in front on the eye while practicing Zen or chanting, either with open or closed eyes. This color dream or image can be a prediction of past, present, or future from a spirit or God.

Don't be frightened if the following happens – your watch stops, electronic equipment stops functioning, you get in an elevator and it stops – all these are indications of abundant chi energy that is unevenly distributed. For ten years any alarm clock placed by my head broke. I finally confessed to my wife. The clock is on her side now and works perfectly.

If beginners practice more than one hour of Chi Gong per day, most of them will feel flu like symptoms within two weeks, it will last two or three days.

If one practices Chi Gong more than three hours per day, within six months one may feel Chi energy flow thru the spine and a chilly feeling coming out through the bones. This is one small success.

Some beginners complain that they can hear someone whispering from across the street and feel very uncomfortable. But it is a temporary symptom.

During Chi energy exchange among students, when one student covers over with two palms to two palms of another student without touching and both eyes closed, sometimes some students will feel images of the bones of the receiver. But it is not clear and happens only temporarily, not every time. Chi Gong masers, Yogis, who are stay in a cave for more than ten years can see the bone and internal organs clearly. Also, they can hear voices of other people from a long distance.

After 6 months of at least 2 to 3 hours per day of training, sometimes you can feel a sick person near you and their sickness may affect your organ. In other words, someone's stomach sickness may affect your stomach, too. I had a 45-year-old student. She came for acupuncture and she said that she had pain in the left lateral side of her leg muscle for three days. I had that pain by wrong exercise three days earlier. She felt it at the same time. One day she came and said that she had diarrhea the day before. My wife had had diarrhea then, too. Her body responded to our sickness or pain. It is a temporary symptom and will go away within a few months.

Shang Hai Chi Gong school required a person who wanted to become an instructor of Chi Gong to stand with a horse stance and do finger exercise for at least four hours per day.

When I was in high school, I read Shakyamuni Buddha's life story and his philosophy. All his teachings made sense, but I did not understand his simplified saying that "one's life is Born, Get Old, Sick and Die." It was such a simple truth. When I was 50 years old, I had a chance to visit a retired pastor in a hospital who was suffering from a stroke. I spoke with him for a while and I learned from him that all human beings wished to "Be Born, Get Old and Die." Everyone wants to skip the Sickness. People like to claim "I was a pastor, priest, doctor, teacher, philanthropist and dedicated follower of religion. Why me? I never cheated people. I was honest and lived a clean lifestyle? Why not you/someone else?"

I knew that a few people get old and die without any medical complications. I think some Taoist, Buddhis, Christian, Catholic, other religions' priests, monks, Yogi, and very few of their followers are born, get old and die.

If you practice Chi Gong and are treated with Oriental medicine, you may less get sickness and suffering when you get old compared to other people who are treated by Western medicine only.

A martial arts organization's junior member and a friend of mine was a head of the educational department of one Christian organization. He visited me in Boston and asked me if I could teach Christian pastors about mild exorcism. He said that a Catholic priest took ten high school or college students to a retreat for meditation and prayer for a weekend.

One or two of the ten students showed symptoms of spirit possession after 2 or 3 days. They were murmuring to themselves or hearing strange voices and showing abnormal behavior. So, the Catholic church appointed a priest who had exorcising ability to take students to a retreat.

I told him that I do it with my students or acupuncture clients for mild cases. I am not able to do it with severe cases. It may be possible that If I was not married and had dedicated my life to only Chi Gong and Oriental medicine that I could. Also, it takes a few months to teach Christian pastors on exorcism.

Generally, Christian pastors have much less experience with fasting than Buddhist priests. I like to suggest to all Christian pastors that they should fast for 10 days after ending of their freshman year of Bible college, after the end of the sophomore year for 20 days, after ending their junior year for 30 days and after the end of the senior year for 40 days.

After Jesus Christ fasted for 40 days, he was tempted by Satan as in New Testament in the Bible. It can happen any time during fasting, even after a single day. If a Bible college wants to teach fasting, It should have a good connection with Catholic church with a priest who can perform exorcism.

Doing excessive Chi Gong practice or not a gradual enough progress and starting and ending each session without meditation can cause people to end up with spirit possession.

The front part of this book mentioned 21 days of fasting by North Korean spies in a cave. Probably 10 percent of soldiers may show symptoms of spirit possession after 21 days of fasting.

CHAPTER 5
Taoists I Have Met

A cave is a sanctuary for Taoists to protect them from the weather and animals. As they describe it, it is a place where no human, dog, or rooster sounds are heard. People feel comfortable and secure when they are in a cave, probably because our ancestors lived in them for long periods of time. Even if there is radon and other gases in a cave it will not affect the health of a Taoist because he/she practices Chi Gong.

If one practices Chi Gong and Zen Meditation in a cave for twelve years, one will be able to see his/her own skeleton and organs and those of others. After ten years of training in a cave, the last test is to put the cave dweller in a cell for ten days without food or water, and only spray water in the room three times a day. The cave dweller should be able to consume the vapor through the nose and lungs to survive. If a man does not drink water for three days, his intestines will dry up and stick together, and he will suffer from Kung Fu. Not so with a serious Chi Gong practitioner.

The 1993 earthquake in San Francisco trapped a person under a highway for five days before being rescued. His kidneys had failed, and he needed a transplant.

I met a Zen Buddhist priest when I was in high school. He was about 70 years old and looked as though he was in his 40s with eyes as clear as a lake and a face with a healthy red color. During one summer vacation period, five of my high school friends and I joined him in his visits of Buddhist Temples in the Korean mountains. We became very tired climbing the high mountains with our packs filled with books, water and a blanket. We stopped to drink and rest. We sweat like rain, as the Koreans describe it, but the priest did not sweat, hunger, or thirst, nor did he get tired. He walked as easily as one would walk on a flat landing strip.

One day he woke us up early in the morning. There was a heavy mist covering the mountain pass. He waved his hands to push the mist away and guided us through the pass. We asked each day after that for him to show us more of his skills, but he refused, though one night he covered the shining stars with a cloud and then moved it away.

My Cha Ryuk (Korean style martial arts and Chi Gong Master) held a demonstration where a busload of 50 passengers ran over his stomach. Sometimes about 20 students would jump at him to kick, punch, pull or push his 140 lb. body, but no one could budge him.

In the early 1980s, a 70-year-old Korean Zen Master climbed near Mount Everest. Everyone else, including the guides, used oxygen tanks except him. Sometimes he rested and took a nap while hanging on a rope while climbing up a cliff.

People who live in high altitudes like the Andes and Himalayans have a higher red blood cell count than people who live in lower levels near sea level. Sue, one of my Chi Gong students, toured Tibet in September of 1998. She went over 17,000 feet, about 6,000 meters.

In the city of Lhasa, 13,000 feet, tourists from all over the world bought oxygen cans in the hotel store. One Japanese tourist collapsed in the lobby. However, I trained Sue before the trip to be able to adapt to the high altitude and she was fine. She did not wake up in the middle of the night gasping for air as if drowning as her companions did. She also taught some of her companions the breathing technique and it helped them too.

Most Chi Gong Masters are not affected by the heat or cold, by dampness or dryness, high or low altitude, hunger or thirst. It does not matter if they wear light or heavy clothing, have material things or not, even have sex or are celibate. They are in a stage beyond that of ordinary people's life standards.

I met a Buddhist priest who can call bugs and scatter them through chanting. I also met a Taoist who can call reptiles like snakes and frogs to exchange cold and warm chi – yin/yang. Some Taoists can tell the direction of the sun or moon while in a dark cave. I heard of a Taoist who could make it rain or stop raining but I have never met anyone who could do that.

While Jesus was praying on a hill, his disciples saw the prophet Elijah and Moses appear beside him, as related in the Bible. My grandmother told me about one of our ancestors, who had appeared in a mountain in North Korea for the last 300 years. He has a big red dot on his cheek and wears a white robe. He has helped people who were lost or chased by animals. Sometimes he calls out the names of our relatives' children and sends his regards. Someday, I will visit this mountain and call out his name so I can meet him.

禪

Chan

Zen Meditation

CHAPTER 6
Charts of Acupuncture Channels

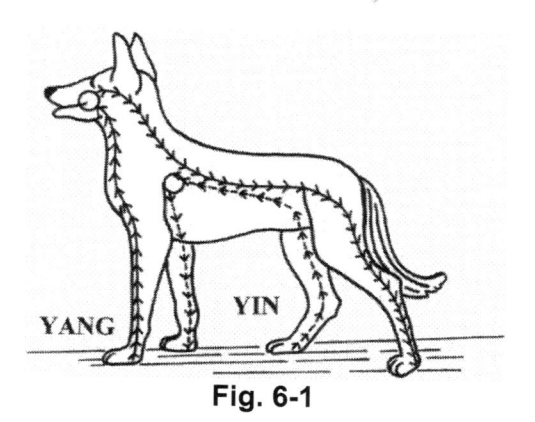

Fig. 6-1

An animal's back – the Yang side (dorsal, posterior part) – is always exposed to sunlight, the heat, wind, rain and snow. It is covered by stronger, thicker muscle layers and hair than the Yin side (ventral, anterior part). It is similar to humans. If someone throws an object at you, such as rocks or a bucket of water, you will shield or cover the front Yin side of your body with your arms, or turn your back – animal instinct at work.

When another person touches us, we are more easily sexually aroused when our Yin part is touched, rather than our Yang parts. Experience teaches a veterinarian that when first touching an animal, they should touch their Yang part; otherwise, an animal will get defensive and act accordingly.

The energy of a Yang channel runs from the hands to the head, then meets the other Yang channels at the head, then goes through the torso to the feet. For example, the Yang channel of the large intestine starts at Large Intestine #1 at the index fingers, and then the chi goes to the head and meets the Yang channels of the stomach. The chi then goes through the torso, legs and into the second toes.

The Yin chi takes a different course. It runs from the toes to the chest, where it meets other Yin channels. The chi then flows through the arms, hands, and fingers. For example, the Yin channel of the spleen starts at Spleen #1 at the big toes, goes through the legs and then the chest at Spleen #21. Here it meets the Yin channel of the Lung under the clavicle area at Lung #1, where the chi then goes through the arms, hand and thumbs at Lung #11.

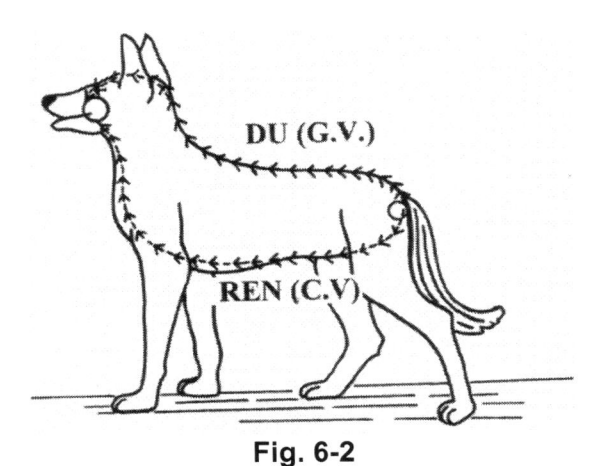

Fig. 6-2

Du channel's Yang energy flows from the tail bone to the top of the head, and then to the upper lip area. This is the opposite direction of the Yang channels. The Yin energy of the Ren channel flows from the anus area to the lower part of the lip, where it there meets the Du channel.

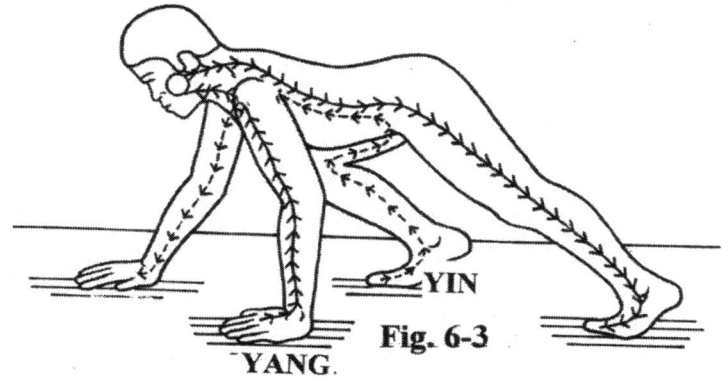

Fig. 6-3
YIN
YANG

The chi flow of a human is the same of an animal, as shown in Figure 6-1 and 6-3.

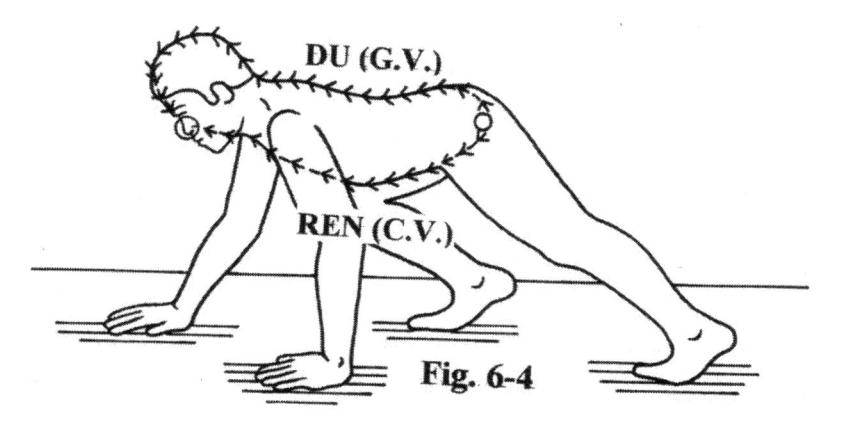

DU (G.V.)
REN (C.V.)
Fig. 6-4

The chi flow of a human is the same of an animal, as shown in Figure 6-2 and 6-4.

CHANNEL PATHWAYS OF TRADITIONAL ORIENTAL MEDICINE
BIOLOGICAL CHI CIRCULATION CLOCK OF EACH CHANNEL

THE LUNG CHANNEL

The Lung Channel originates in the middle of the body and runs down internally to connect with the large intestine (A). It then turns upward, passing by the stomach (B) and through the diaphragm (C) before entering the lungs (D). From here, it rises to the throat and then emerges to the surface at Lu#1 under the clavicle. The Lung Channel runs externally down the medial aspect of the arm, passes by the radial artery at the wrist, and ends at the medial side of the tip of the thumb at Lu 11. A connecting channel runs from Lu#7 near the wrist (above the styloid process of the radius) to the radial side of the tip of the index finger, where it links to the Large Intestine Channel. (see Figure 6-5). **(4-6 AM)**

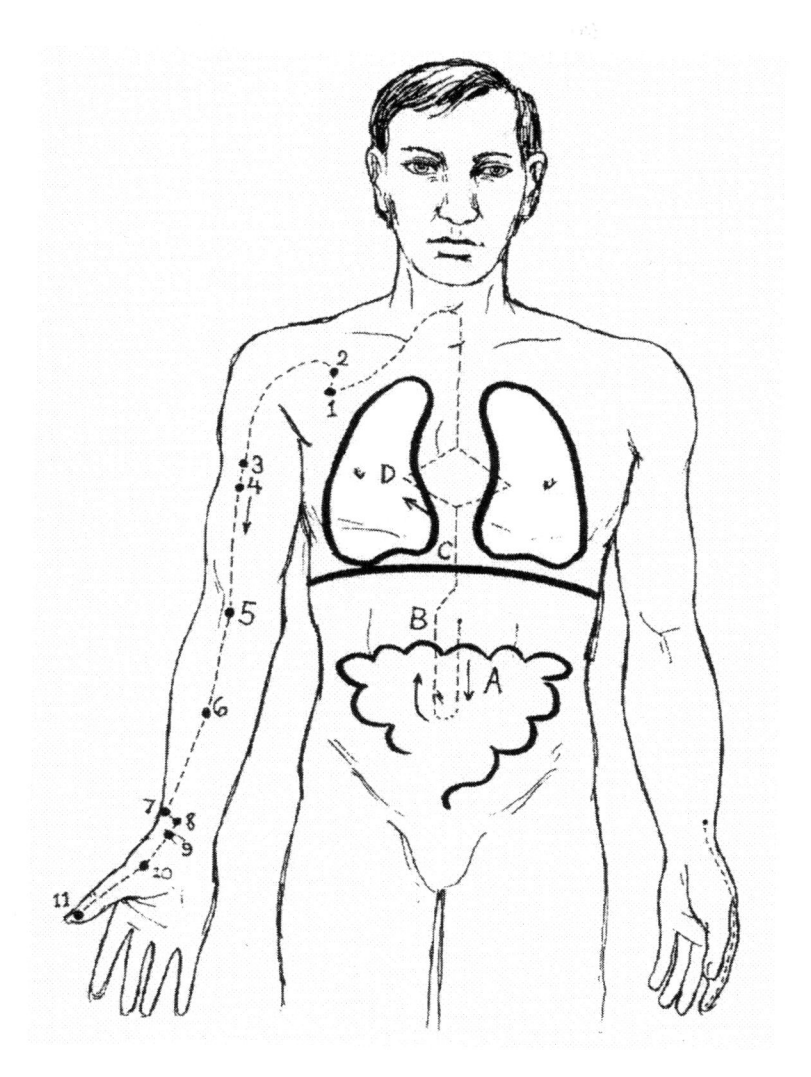

**Hand Tai Yin
Lung Channel
Fig. 6-5**

THE LARGE INTESTINE CHANNEL

The Large Intestine Channel begins at the tip of the index finger (LI#1) and runs up along its radial side. It then ascends along the lateral-anterior aspect of the arm to the highest point of the shoulder (LI#15). From here, it passes to the seventh cervical vertebra where it connects with Du#14 (A) and then crosses to the front of the body above the collarbone. At this point, the Channel divides into two branches.

The internal branch connects downwards to the lungs (B), the diaphragm (C), and the large intestine (D). The external branch ascends along the neck to the cheek from where it enters the gums of the lower teeth. It crosses the upper lip to the opposite side of the body and ends at the side of the nose (LI#20), where it connects to the Stomach Channel (see Figure 6-6). **(6-8 AM)**

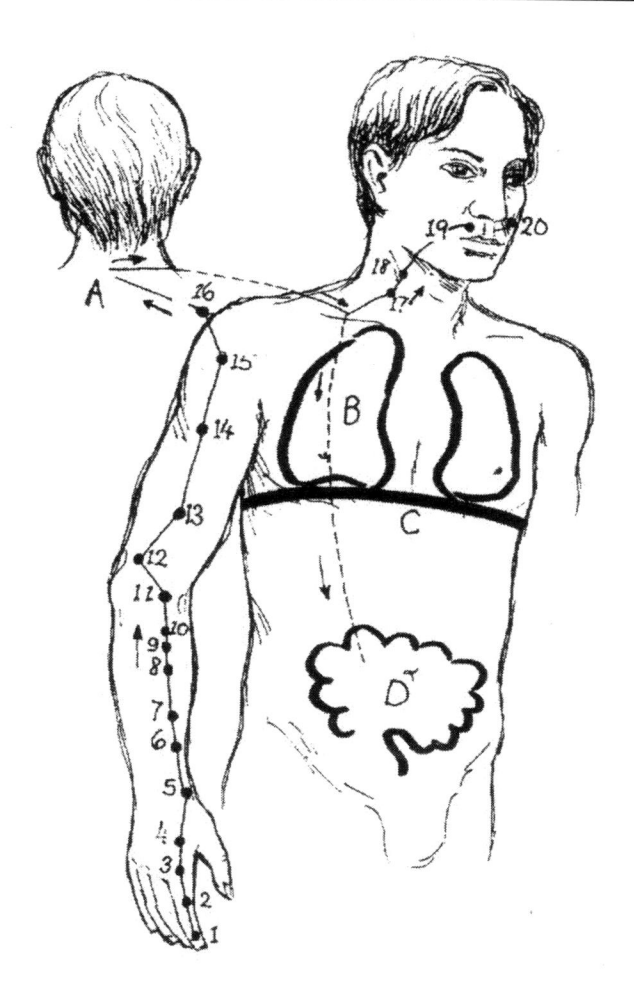

**Hand Yang Ming
Large Intestine Channel
Fig. 6-6**

THE STOMACH CHANNEL

The Stomach Channel begins internally at the side of the nose. It ascends the bridge of the nose and connects with the Urinary Bladder Channel at the inner corner of the eye (UB#1). It emerges below the eyeball (St#1) and then descends, entering the upper gums and curving around the lips. From under the mouth it follows the lower jaw, then turning upward passes in front of the ear to the forehead.

From St#5 the channel runs down along the throat to the area above the collarbone. An internal branch descends from there through the diaphragm (A), entering the stomach (B), and connecting with the spleen (C).

The external branch runs downward along the chest, passing through the nipple and past the umbilicus to the groin (St#30). At this point, it reconnects with the internal channel. From here, the channel descends the front of the leg all the way to the lateral side of the second toe.

There are two branches below the knee. One runs from just below the knee (St#36) to the lateral side of the middle toe. The second leaves from the top of the foot (St#42) and connects to the Spleen Channel at the medial side of the big toe (see Figure 6-7). **(8-10 AM)**

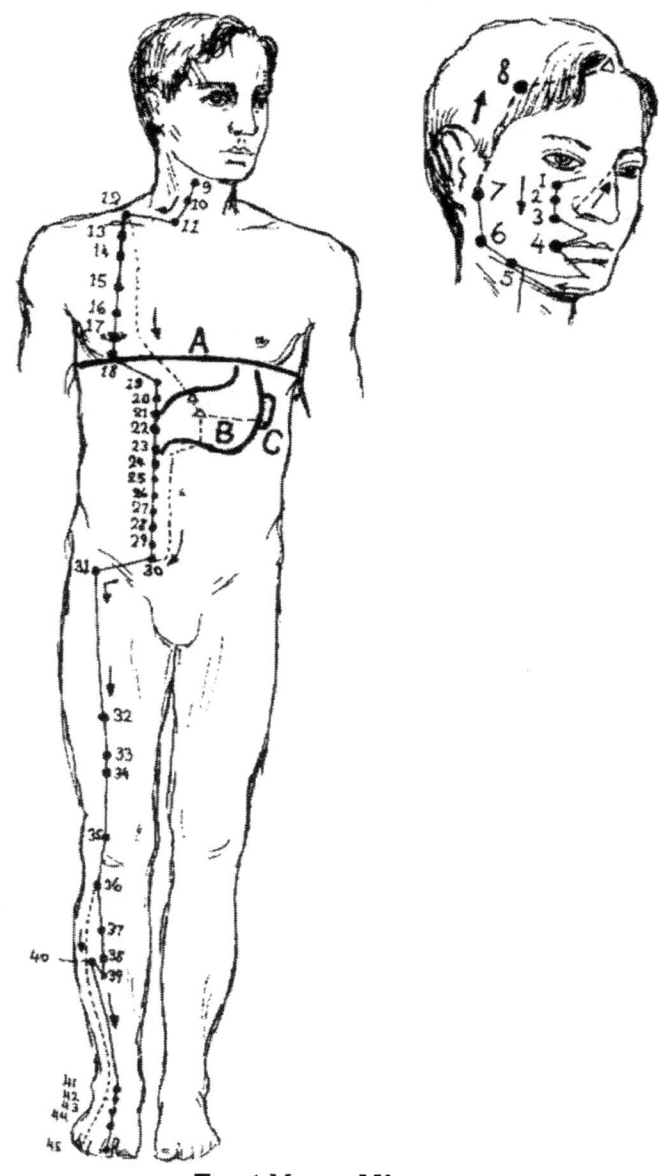

Foot Yang Ming
Fig. 6-7 Stomach Channel

SPLEEN CHANNEL

The Spleen Channel begins on the inside of the big toe (Sp#1) and runs along the inside of the foot, turning upwards in front of the inner ankle. It then ascends along the inside of the leg to the abdomen. At Sp#15, lateral to the umbilicus, an internal pathway connects with the spleen (A) and the stomach (B) and then runs up through the diaphragm (C) to the heart (D), where the Spleen and Heart Channels connect.

The main channel continues to ascend to the chest, and from Sp#20 another internal pathway runs upward through the throat and terminates on the lower surface of the tongue. The main channel descends from Sp#20 and ends at Sp#21 on the side of the rib cage (see Figure 6-8). **(10 to 12 Noon)**

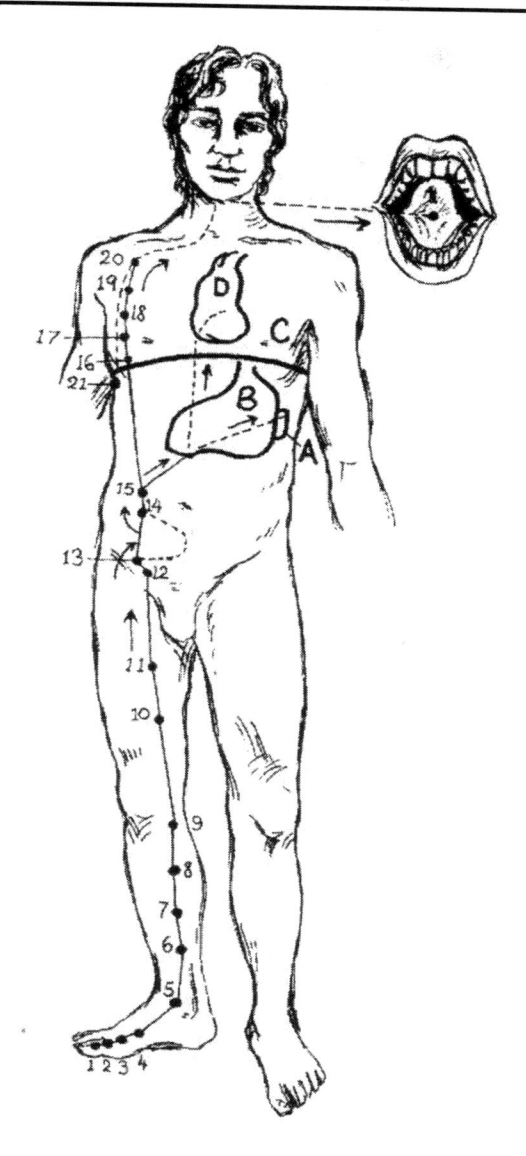

**Foot Tai Yin
Spleen Channel
Fig. 6-8**

HEART CHANNEL

The Heart Channel originates in the heart (A). Three internal branches begin there. One runs downward through the diaphragm and connects with the small intestine (B). A second runs upward through the throat to the eye (C). The third passes through the lungs (D) and emerges at Ht#1 in the armpit. The external channel then descends along the medial side of the arm and terminates on the inside tip of the little finger at Ht #9, where it connects with the Small Intestine Channel (see Figure 6-9). **(12 Noon- 2 PM)**

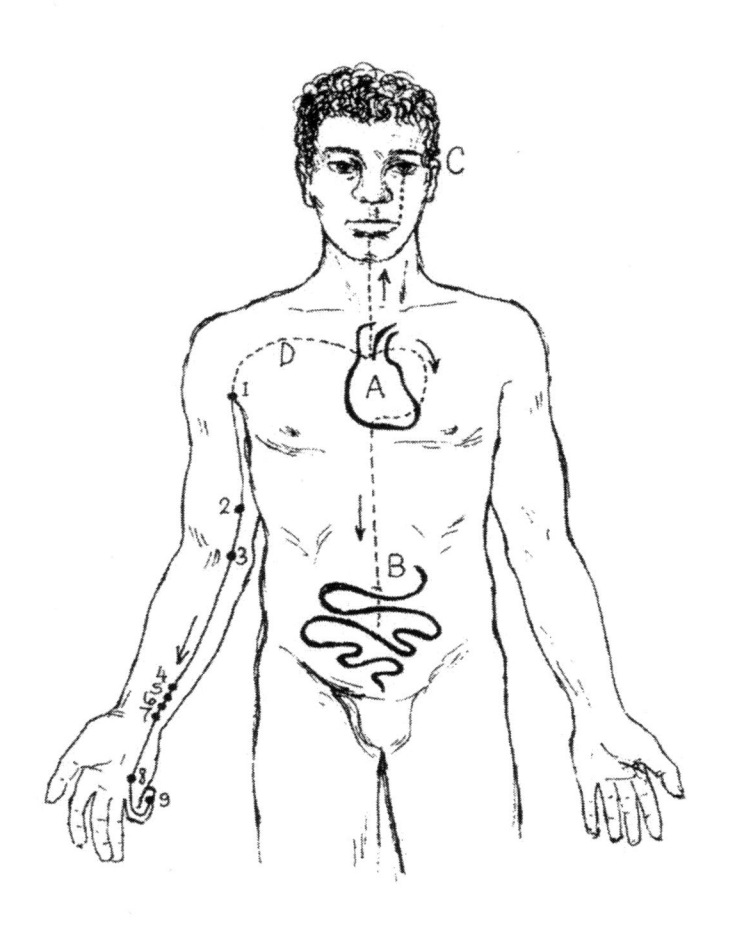

Hand Shao Yin
Heart Channel
Fig. 6-9

SMALL INTESTINE CHANNEL

The Small Intestine Channel begins on the outside of the tip of the little finger at SI#1. It ascends along the inside of the back of the hand and the posterior aspect of the arm to the back of the shoulder joint. From there it runs to the center of the upper back where it connects with Du 14 (A) and then crosses to the front of the body. An internal branch separates above the collar bone and descends through the heart (B), the diaphragm (C), and the stomach (D), before terminating at the small intestine (E).

The external channel ascends along the neck to the cheek, from where it connects to the ear, where the channel ends at SI 19. A branch runs from SI#18 on the cheek to the inner corner of the eye, where it connects with the Urinary Bladder Channel (see Figure 6-10).
(2-4 PM)

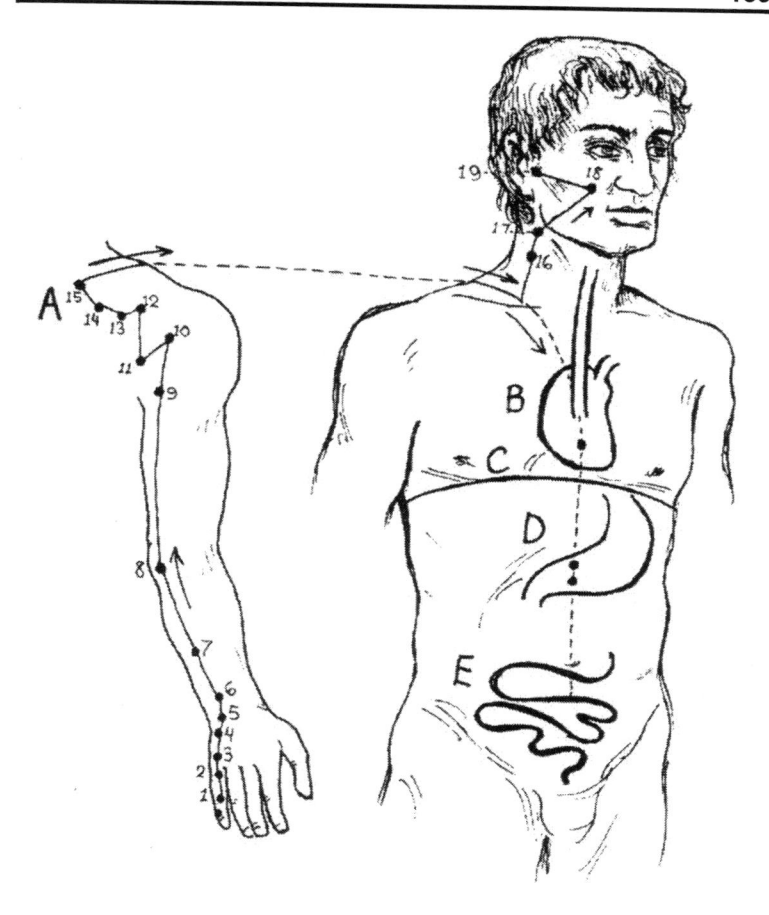

Fig. 6-10

**Hand Tai Yang
Small Intestine Channel**

URINARY BLADDER CHANNEL

The Urinary Bladder Channel starts at the inner corner of the eye and ascends the forehead to the vertex of the head (A), where it connects to Du#20. It then descends along the back of the head and divides in two at the back of the neck.

Both branches continue to descend parallel to the spine. The inner branch has an internal connection that originates in the lumbar region and enters the kidney (B) and the urinary bladder (C). The inner branch continues down through the buttocks and the back of the thigh to the back of the knee (D).

The outer branch follows the same course as the inner branch down the back but is further from the spine (E). It connects to the Gall Bladder Channel on the buttocks at GB#30 (F) and reunites with the inner branch behind the knee at UB#40.

From here the single channel runs down the back of the calf (G) and around the outside ankle bone, then along the outside of the foot to the outside tip of the little toe at UB#67, where it connects with the Kidney Channel (see Figure 6-11).
(4-6 PM)

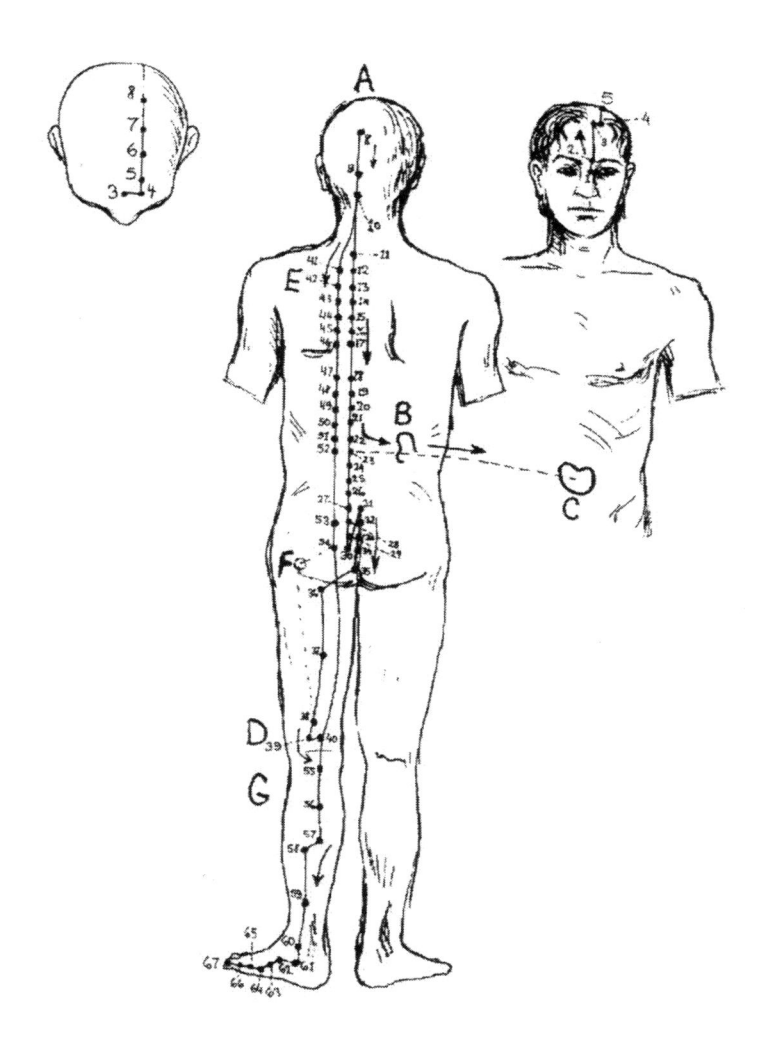

**Foot Tai Yang
Urinary Bladder Channel
Fig. 6-11**

KIDNEY CHANNEL

The Kidney Channel starts on the underside of the little toe and runs along the sole of the foot (K#1). From there it runs under the navicular bone and behind the inner ankle. Then it ascends the inner side of the leg to the top of the thigh (A). An internal branch runs from here to the base of the spine (A) where it connects to Du#1. The internal branch then ascends along the lumbar spine and enters the kidney (B) and the urinary bladder (C). Another internal branch runs from the kidney up to the liver (D), the diaphragm (E), the lung (F), and continues through the throat to the base of the tongue (G). The main channel ascends from the inner thigh up the abdomen and the chest to the collarbone where it ends at K#27. From the lung, a branch joins the heart and flows into the chest where it connects with the Pericardium Channel (see Figure 6-12).

(6-8 PM)

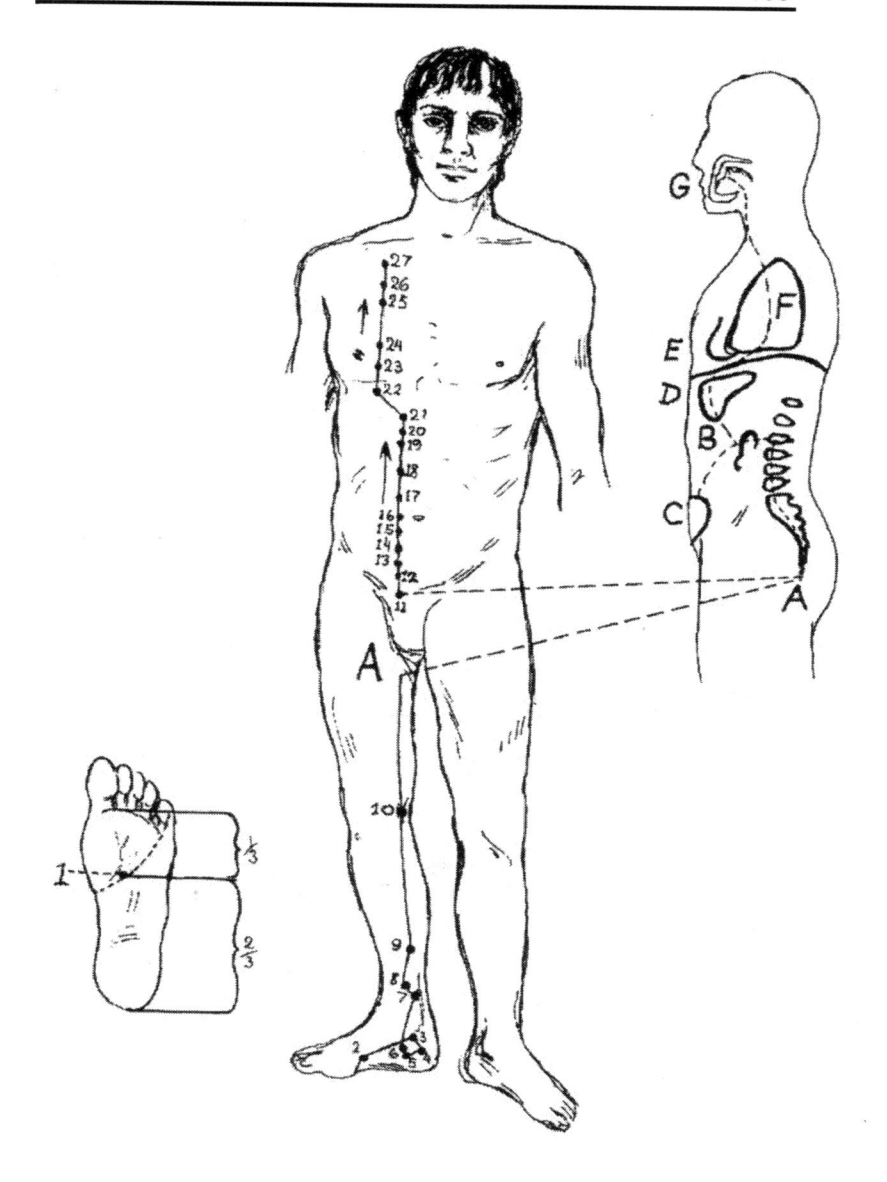

**Foot Shao Yin
Kidney Channel
Fig. 6-12**

PERICARDIUM CHANNEL

The Pericardium Channel originates in the chest and enters the pericardium (A). An internal branch descends through the diaphragm (B) to the abdomen (C), connecting with the Upper, Middle, and Lower portions of the Triple Warmer. Another internal branch runs from the middle of the chest to an area just lateral to the nipple where it emerges at P#1.

The external channel runs from here through the armpit and then down the medial aspect of the arm all the way to the palm of the hand at P#8. From this point the main channel extends to the tip of the middle finger where it ends at P#9. A branch runs to the tip of the ring finger, where it connects with the Triple Warmer Channel (see Figure 6-13). **(8-10 pm)**

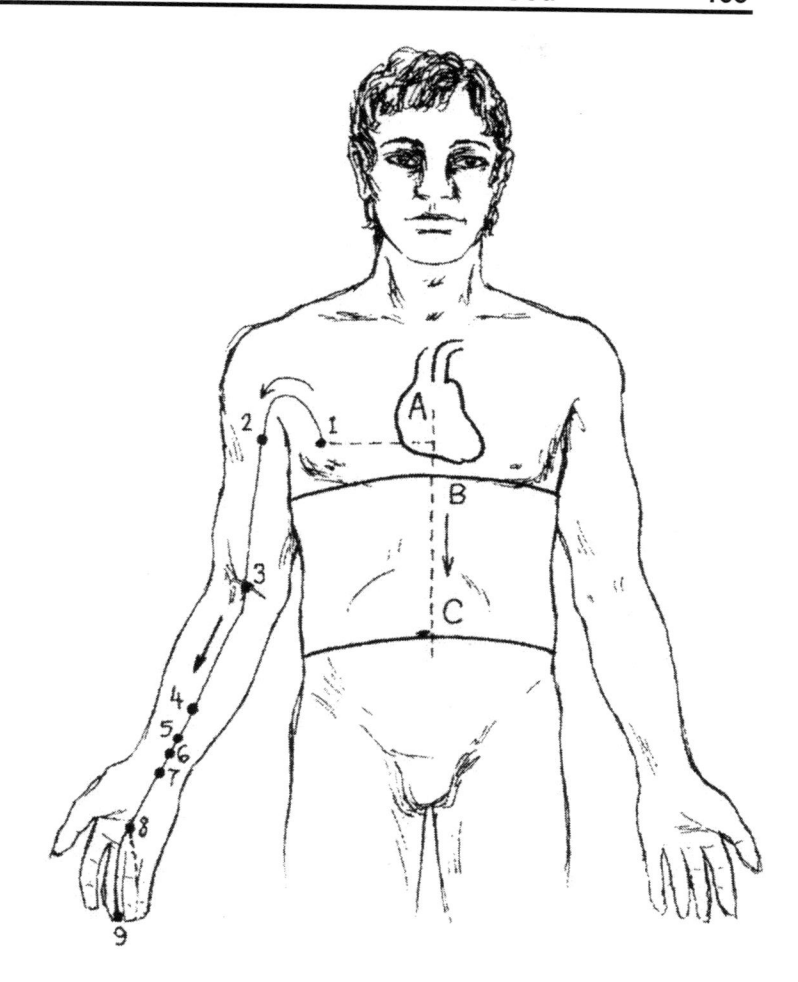

Fig. 6-13

**Hand Jue Yin
Pericardium Channel**

TRIPLE WARMER

The Triple Warmer Channel originates at the tip of the ring finger (TW#1) and runs between the fourth and fifth metacarpal bones, then over the wrist and up the back of the arm to the shoulder joint at TW#14. From here it goes across the back of the shoulder (A) where it connects with the Gall Bladder Channel at GB#21. The channel then crosses to the front of the body. An internal branch enters the chest to connect with the pericardium (B) and then descends through the diaphragm (C) and down to the abdomen (D), linking the Upper, Middle, and Lower Warmers.

The external channel ascends along the side of the neck to the base of the ear (TW#17), from where it circles behind the ear, then turns downward to the cheek and terminates at TW#23 at the outer corner of the eye, where it connects to the Gall Bladder Channel. An internal branch on the face runs from TW#20 above the ear up onto the head and then descends along the temple before connecting with SI#18 below the eye (see Figure 6-14).
(10 PM - 12 Midnight)

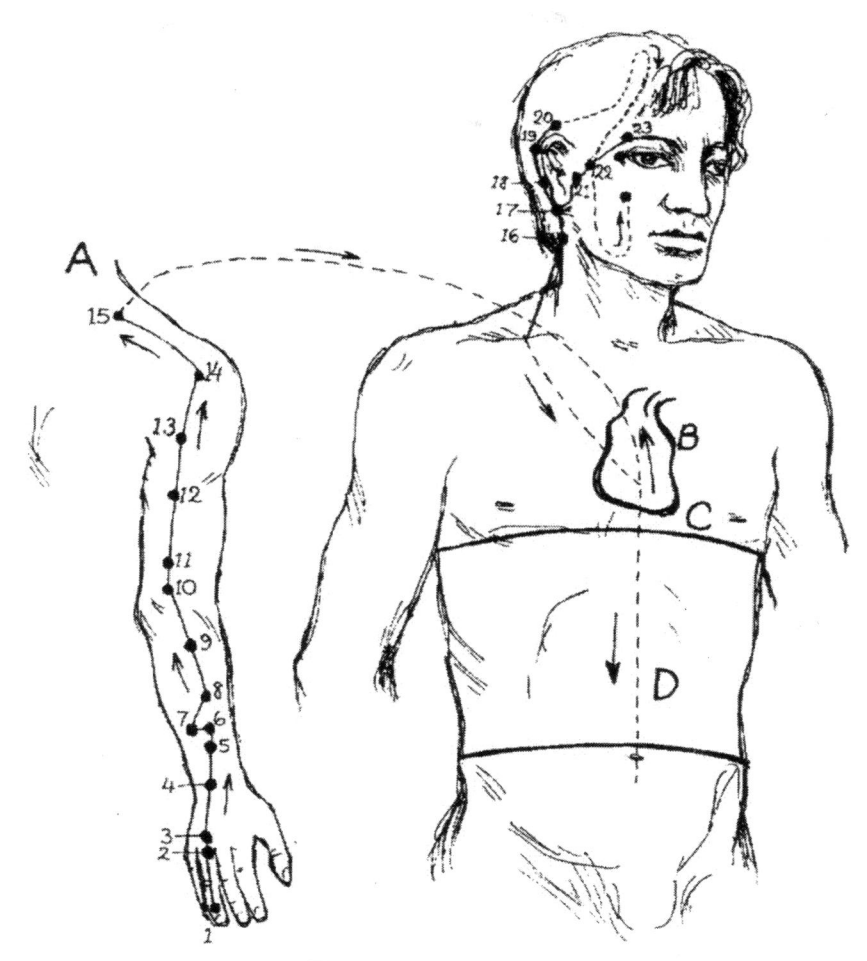

Fig. 6-14
Hand Shao Yang
Triple Warmer Channel

GALL BLADDER CHANNEL

The Gall Bladder Channel begins at the outer corner of the eye at GB#1. From here an internal branch descends through the neck and the chest through the diaphragm to the liver (A) and the gall bladder (B). It then continues downward along the side of the abdomen and connects with the main channel on the side of the buttock (C) at GB#30.

The external channel ascends to the corner of the forehead (GB#4), circles behind the ear (GB#12), then returns to the forehead (GB#14), before descending to the back of the neck and the top of the shoulder (GB#21). An internal branch runs from here to the back, connecting with Du#14, UB#11, and SI#12. From the top of the shoulder the main channel descends (D) in front of the armpit and along the side of the chest and torso to the hip where it intersects the internal branch at GB#30.

The single channel then descends along the outside of the leg, passes in front of the outer ankle and over the back of the foot before ending at GB#44 on the outside of the fourth toe. From GB#41 on the back of the foot, a branch crosses over to the big toe, where it connects with the Liver Channel (see Figure 6-15). **(12 midnight - 2 AM)**

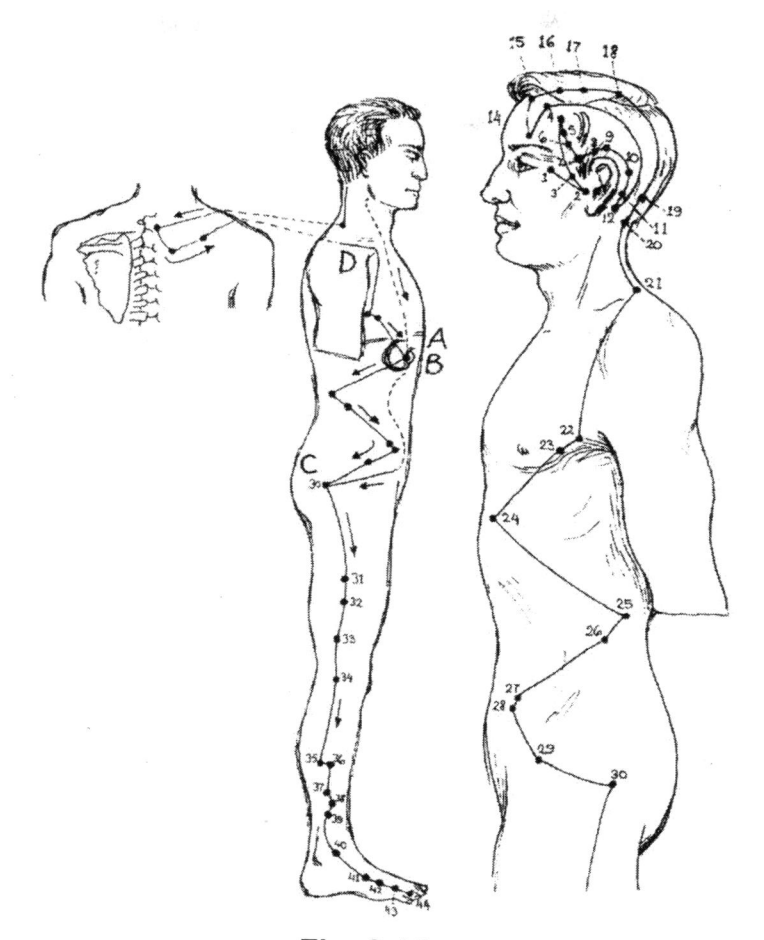

Fig. 6-15

**Foot Shao Yang
Gall Bladder Channel**

LIVER CHANNEL

The Liver Channel begins on the top of the big toe and runs upward along the back of the foot to the front of the inside ankle. It then ascends the inside of the leg until it reaches the genital region. After encircling the genitals, it runs up the abdomen until it reaches LIV#13 below the rib cage, where an internal branch separates. The main external channel then terminates at LIV#14 below the nipple.

The internal branch enters the liver (A) and connects with the gall bladder (B). It then ascends, crossing the diaphragm (C) and entering the lungs (D) where it connects with the Lung Channel and completes the cycle. An internal branch continues upwards from here through the throat to the eye (E) and then up to the vertex of the head. Another branch descends from the eye to encircle the mouth (see Figure 6-16). **(2-4 AM)**

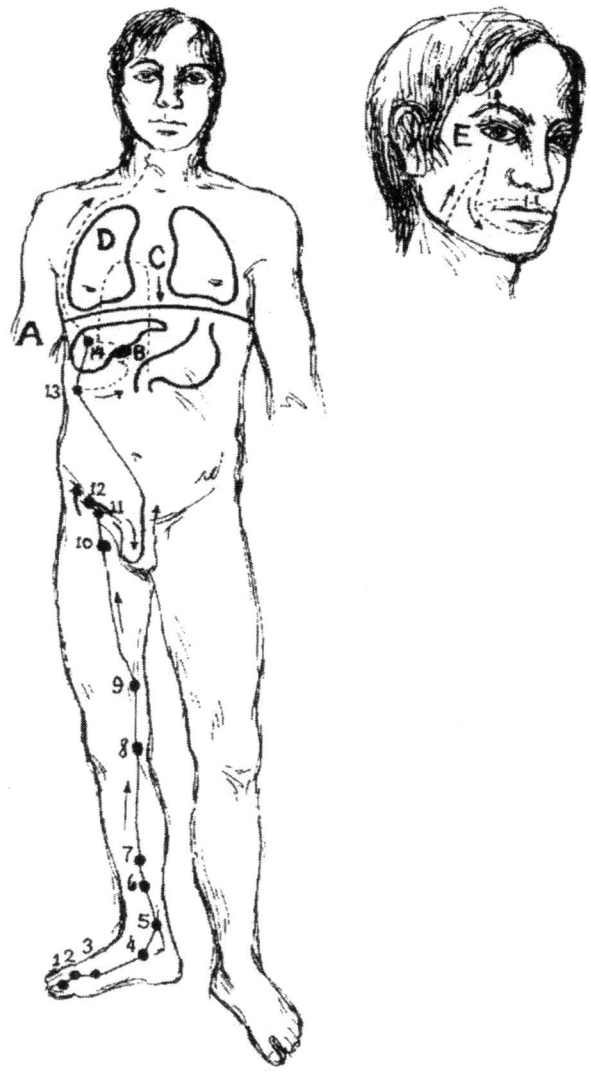

Fig. 6-16

**Foot Jue Yin
Liver Channel**

DU (Governing Vessel) CHANNEL

The Du Channel begins in the lower abdomen and descends internally to emerge at Du#1 between the anus and the coccyx. It then ascends the midline of the back and the head to the vertex (Du#20) from where it descends across the forehead and the tip of the nose before ending at Du#28 inside the upper lip (see Figure 6-17).

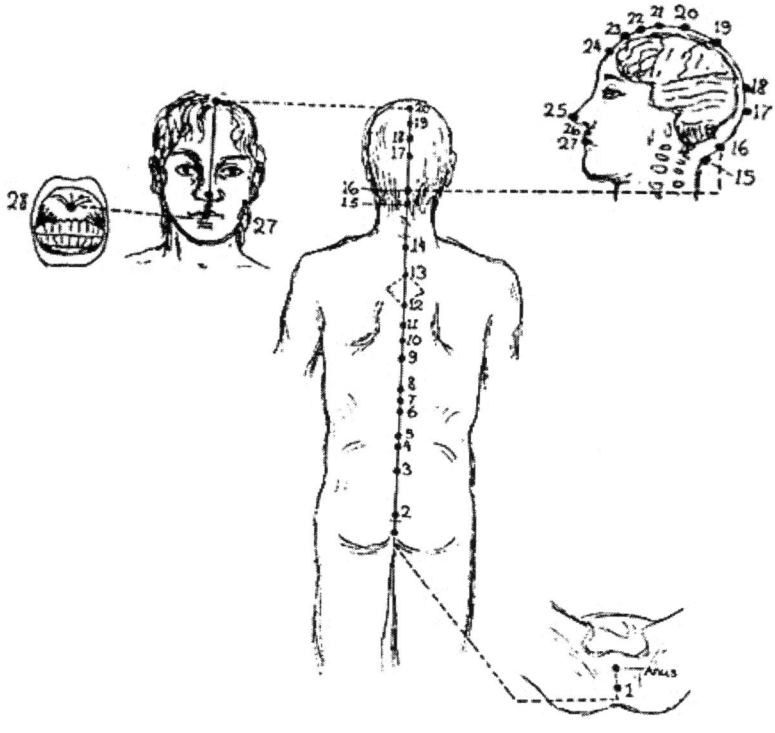

Fig. 6-17
Governing Vessel
DU Channel

REN (CV) CHANNEL

The Ren Channel begins in the lower abdomen and descends internally before emerging at REN#1 between the anus and the genitals. It then ascends along the midline of the abdomen and chest before ending at REN#24 below the lower lip. Internal pathways from this point encircle the lips and extend upwards to St#1 just below the eyes (see Figure 6-18).

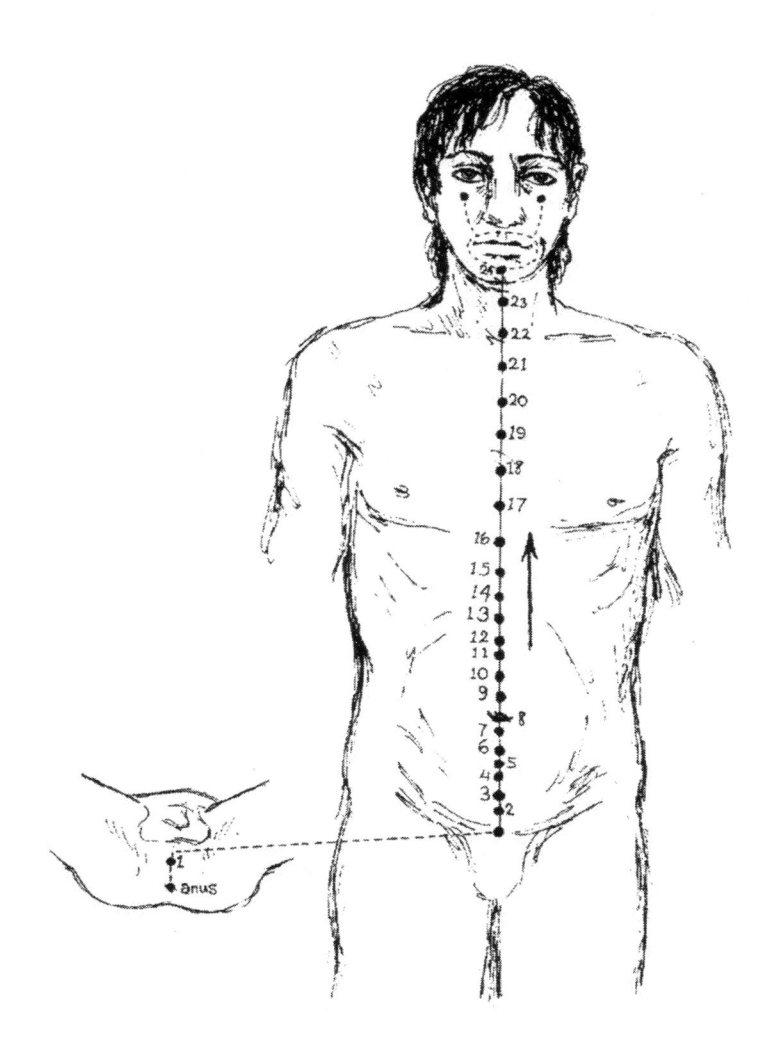

Fig. 6-18

**CV
REN Channel**

五行

WU   **HSING**

Five Element Theory

CHAPTER 7
Cautions to Note While Practicing Chi Gong

The most difficult art to teach is Chi Gong. It is not like other sports or martial arts. In this practice, the student can be faced with physical or emotional problems. A Chi Gong Master should have the ability and experience to solve the problems.

Chi Gong masters must be able to treat chi stagnation by hand or with acupuncture and even be able to perform an exorcism, if necessary. Also, the Master must be capable of moving chi or infusing a client with chi better than an ordinary acupuncturist.

Do not mix external styles and internal styles of martial arts or Chi Gong. Most Olympic sports, Tae Kwon Do and Karate, jumping, running and fast-breathing types of style develop muscles. It is much different form Chi Gong. Both styles should not be mixed.

Internal-style marital artist should fish rather than hunt. Fish in a lake rather than in a deep sea. Listen to soft classical music rather than hard rock. Follow these guidelines for smooth chi circulation.

I met a few external-style marital artist instructors who complained that after Chi Gong practice, they got tired and weaker. Tai Chi and Chi Gong instructors have fewer problems than external-style martial artists who mix both internal and external styles. But sometimes internal style marital artists can be faced with more severe physical and emotional problems or even possessed by a spirit.

I have met many Tae Kwon Do and Karate instructors who practice Chi Gong these days. It is important to build up and save chi energy, but how to circulate the energy is equally important.

One who builds up chi energy and stores it in their own body, then teaches sports or external style marital arts – moving fast, yelling loudly, lifting weights – will disturb their chi flow. This can cause many problems, including physical pain, tiredness, anxiety, depression and insomnia.

It is ideal not to practice any external style exercise at all while practicing Chi Gong. But if you do light jogging, calisthenics, fewer than 30 push-ups and sit ups, or light muscle work, building up slowly and over time, it will not interfere greatly with your Chi Gong practice.

A few years ago, I taught a 35-year-old male student. He complained about numb, painful, and shaking hands over the last 10 years. He said there were no Doctors of western medicine that could diagnose or help him. I asked many questions and checked his body for surgery scars, sports injuries, inquired about possible car accidents, spinal/neck/lumbar problems, and looked for any blocked channels but there was no evidence of any of this. His body and mental state were both normal. After much questioning, I found that he had practiced a Chinese martial art form. "Iron Palm Technique." He had hit a bean bag the size of a sofa pillow a few hundred times each session with the palms of his hand, then washed his hands with an herbal ointment called "Dit Da Jow, or Tai Chi Yu." When he broke bricks with his palm he contracted and held his breath. He also practiced an internal- style breathing technique for many years. So, his breathing was internal, and his style was external.

The chi stored in his body was blocked by pounding the bean bag very hard with the palm, and this caused pain, numbness and shaking. I advised him to pick one style and do it for one year. I would like to advise anyone who is over 35 years and wants to develop the Iron Palm technique to do an internal style.

Cautions to Note While Practicing Chi Gong

One should practice the pushing technique of Tai Chi, or the pushing up and down movement illustrated in **Figs 3-17 through 3-20** from Chapter 3, with slow breathing and a consciousness of *chi* flow.

Another good practice to learn is Bagua Palm. One should do this a few hundred times a day or at least one hour per day for ten years to reach the goal. Practicing Chi Gong at the same time, it will shorten the time.

Chi Gong practitioners should not drink alcohol. A few years ago, Chi Gong devotees in Europe gathered at an annual celebration in Madrid, Spain. They drank and danced to rock music. Some danced like a dog, a monkey, a bear, horse or tiger. It was possible that they were possessed by an animal spirit or showed an indication of their former life. It is possible never to wake up and stay like an animal forever. This is a mad state. This is a very dangerous practice and shows the ignorance of the Chi Gong practitioners.

One of my Chi Gong students was in a hospital lobby, waiting for a friend who was in the ER. This, as many of us know, can mean a wait of several hours. So, my student decided to practice Chi Gong while he was waiting, standing in front of a plant and breathing. Later he realized that many security guards were standing behind him and waiting to jump him, probably thinking he was drunk or mad. So, I now advise my students not to frighten others when they practice, unless they are so advanced that they can walk out of a mental ward like an invisible man, like a Taoist priest, Yogi, or a magician such as Harry Houdini.

When I lived in North Carolina in 1989, a Native American visited my clinic and asked me to help his 12-year-old son. He couldn't speak a word, but made animal sounds and crawled on his hands and knees like an infant.

This man had brought his son to many doctors of western medicine including neurologists and psychologists, but no one could help.

He came to me for advice. He did not want to bring his son into my clinic as he acted like an animal. So, one weekend, with much curiosity, I visited his home. When I was greeted by the Native American in his living room, an animal, or something, rapidly crawled towards me and made loud growling noises. I was so frightened that I jumped. The man held his son, who was acting like a bear. I asked the man if he hunted bears. He confessed that he had hunted bears illegally for Korean customers who lived in New York. He explained that when he tried to catch a bear, he tied a dog to a tree. When the bear attacked the dog, he shot the bear. He then removed the bear's gall bladder and threw the rest away. Sometimes he would save the skin, and would also save the claws for the Koreans, who paid much money for the bear's feet.

I asked him about the other ways he earned a living. He said that he had worked as a farmer, construction worker, or made whiskey illegally in the woods – something for which that area of North Carolina was notorious. I then explained to him the history of native Americans and that they believed that an animal has a spirit, just like a human. I advised him to stop hunting bears and earn an honest wage as a farmer or construction worker, even if it meant a lower income.

I told him to live a clean life, or else his son would not be cured and could possibly hurt someone in his family. I told him that if someone hunts bears for something other than a food source, he will face the dead bear spirit or be reborn as a bear. I warned that a future newborn or one of his grandchildren could be possessed by an animal spirit and be born and act like a bear or dog.

I treated the son with an emphasis more on chi energy than acupuncture and prayed for the bear spirit to leave him. Six months later, the son began to walk and spoke like a newborn. I recently heard that he is in Middle School.

Many Koreans try to purchase a bear's gall bladder. It is commonly used for lower back pain and hepatitis. They also believe that it can help control or heal any disease and use it for an aphrodisiac as well. I do not believe the miraculous effect attributed to the gall bladder. Native Americans had used gall bladders as medicine, but they do not use it anymore, and it is also forbidden to sell any animal part like this throughout the world today. However, the illegal market still operates, and a hunter is paid $300 for a bear's gall bladder, which is then sold to the Koreans for $1,000.

In 1992 a Korean newspaper wrote about a wholesaler who smuggled bears' gall bladders into New York City. He was found robbed and murdered in his apartment, with an estimated $20,000 in cash missing. This sounds like just another drug dealer's story.

Anyone who is near death or weakened by old age often is visited by the spirit of a dead friend or relative. The departed loved one will even appear in the daytime. Sometimes old people talk to them. Nurses who observe this at nursing homes simply think the old person is senile, but they are not. This is a natural phenomenon that everyone can experience during his or her lifetime.

In 1993, a 40-year-old woman was in my Chi Gong class for the first time. She said she felt very strong chi and became extremely excited. It was early evening. I advised her to never practice at night just before bed. Three days later, she returned and told me that she could not sleep for 3 nights and that when she would close her eyes, her skeleton and internal organs appeared in front of her.

I gave her chi energy to direct her chi flow, and after treatment, I told her that if this persisted for 3 more days, to come back for acupuncture. I have never heard from her again.

As I mentioned earlier, this type of ability typically takes 10 years of practice in a cave to develop. But as I have also previously mentioned, sometimes this ability can happen to women temporarily.

Chi Gong practitioners are sometimes possessed by a good or evil spirit. Jesus met Satan after 40 days of fasting in the wilderness. A practitioner will suffer from it, but an excellent Chi Gong Master is able to take care of the problem.

An instructor taught Chi Gong late in the evening at an acupuncture school. Most of the students vomited, got headaches, or had insomnia. This is what happens to people who practice at nighttime. Practicing late can cause too much chi energy to flow through your body and disturb your sleep.

Whether you practice external or internal exercises like Chi Gong at night, after this you should rub your hands and feet or immerse them in warm-to-hot water for a few minutes, then do the breathing exercises as shown in Figures 3-17 through 3-20 in Chapter 3. This will bring your chi energy down from the head to the navel area (tan tien). You should then practice Zen meditation until sleepy.

If you go to bed just after watching a movie or TV, your body may sleep but your spirit is wide awake and wandering. The same is true after a heavy meal. If you go to sleep right after a heavy meal, you will feel uncomfortable and may not be able to sleep.

Chi Gong Medicine From GOD

Then you should follow the same procedure outlined above, and a few minutes later your stomach will make sounds, a signal of your chi energy moving food from the stomach into the small intestines.

The best way to practice Chi Gong is to check your chi flow regularly and receive chi energy or correct an imbalance with acupuncture. Herbal tea also helps, as does a simple and clean lifestyle, free of a strong materialistic desire. I observed some Chi Gong practitioners suddenly develop or receive tremendous chi energy to become a healer. They would then "show-off" in pursuit of fame and fortune. Sooner or later, their ability would disappear like the morning time mist after the sun rises.

The Taoist's attitude is to purify one's soul and body continually. They do not seek fortune and fame from their chi energy, as they believe that once they obtain the highest level of health possible that they should try to help others. They know that anyone who goes against this Taoist canon will have their ability taken away by God, the creator.

Case 1) A psychiatrist friend of mine referred me to a girl diagnosed with an uncontrollable epileptic seizure. We agreed that this was spirit possession. A 14-year-old girl visited me with her parents. They said that she had panic attacks and showed similar symptoms of epileptic seizures once or twice per month. She said that a big black man with a long tongue attacked her. I treated her with Acupuncture and Chi energy. She felt better. Her parents asked me that what to do next and I told them that she might be very sick that night and the next day and then she might be cured. Otherwise, they should visit me again. They visited a week later. Her parents said that she suffered severely on the first and second days, but since then she seemed to get better.

Jesus Christ expelled a demon spirit from a person and the reaction was very violent. The person fell after the demon spirit left his body. It is written in New Testament of the Holy Bible.

Case 2) A New England Acupuncture school called me and referred two clients who were mentally sick. The next day two ladies visited my clinic. One was about 30 years old with a blank facial expression with no appearance of a soul and another over 40 years old. The second one's face looked like Linda Blair in the 70's Exorcist movie. Before Acupuncture treatment, I let the younger client sit on a chair with hands over her chest and top of her head without touching. I felt not so much irregularity from her. Then, I did the same procedure with the older client. With her I felt very strong chills and an eerie feeling coming from her. I concentrated all my chi energy and prayed to God to expel the bad spirit from her. About 10 minutes later she said that she felt better. I advised the younger lady to watch and take care of her friend through the night for a couple of days.

Five days later the younger client came back and said that she didn't need any more treatment and that her friend was very sick and shaking the first night and that then she had gradually become better. She did not need any more treatment and she moved to California.

Case 3) I treated four 10th grade high school students for their drug addictions. I treated them with Acupuncture and Chi Gong.

Jason was a good patient for following my Chi Gong instruction and lifestyle adjustment beside acupuncture treatment. He recommended me to his friends. He became an acupuncturist after graduating from high school and Acupuncture college. Jason's friend Mike was in a mental institution for a month and was later discharged from there.

Jason visited me with Mike. He had short, crew cut hair and had dyed it a silver color. He glared at me with his blue eyes. I let him sit on a chair with his eyes closed. I placed one hand over his head and the other hand over his chest without touching. I felt a very cold and eerie feeling. I felt that I met a strong challenger.

When I opened my eyes, I saw his palms facing towards me. That pose was one of the Buddhist Chi Gong poses and I was going to teach it on the following week at Shiatsu school. He showed off his ability to read my mind even about future plans. I was amazed by that. I put him on an exam table and gave an acupuncture and Chi infusion treatment. I never felt it before – a very cold and eerie feeling. After 30 minutes he said he felt better. I told his friend to bring back him within a week. When they came back, his friend A told me that he was very sick the evening of the treatment. He asked his parents to borrow the car keys to going somewhere. They had hard time calming him down. He never came back after the two treatments.

Jason visited me with his friend named Jeff who was almost like a homeless man. He slept in an old car. He seemed confused and not mentally stable. He said he wanted to become a rapper like a famous rapper in New York City.

He had laid down on an exam table and I performed Acupuncture. Then, I left the room to talk more with his friend. Suddenly we heard a cell phone type buzzing sound. I went to the room and I saw he made a sound by covering his mouth with one hand. It was amazing. He may be qualified to be a rapper. I treated him about four different times and then he wanted to become an assistant instructor for the Kundalini Yoga school.

The head instructor and owner was an Indian lady. But he had a Catholic background and he told me that he had sin in him. So, he thought he was not qualified to become an assistant teacher. I told him that everybody commits minor sin every day. I told him, "You were just an ordinary guy like me. You are qualified enough to be an assistant instructor."

He jumped on a passing train and killed himself while he was walking on a street with his friend A. My regret was that I should have treated him more. I charged him a very low fee for my treatment, and I offered him some free treatment, but he refused it.

Case 4) A 20-year-old man visited me with his psychiatrist and his parents. He had learned Chi Gong from his uncle and had studied it more by video instruction three years earlier. A few months later, every day, he heard a voice repeatedly. It said, "Do not eat." Since then, he could not swallow any food. So, a surgeon made a hole through his throat and inserted food through a tube. I tried to help him, but I had to move to Oklahoma. I suggested to him that he should try to find a Catholic priest who is able to do exorcism.

Two of my close friends and Chi Gong cult members, Master Q and K, visited me in Boston from a Korean mountain in year 2010. I had not seen them for more than fifteen years. They had changed in many ways.

Master Q had done fasting meditation in a cave for 21 days. I mentioned it in the first part of the book. He did it in solitary confinement like in a Buddhist temple during the winter season. During other seasons there were too many insects and mountain hiking people around to disturb him. After he finished 21 days of fasting, he was tempted by an evil spirit, but he could expel it.

During that cold winter in a cave, he started a small bonfire every day, but cold winter breezes came into the cave day and night. He covered the entrance and wall with very thick Styrofoam. It warmed him up during his stay, but he got permanent asthma symptoms. He should have stayed in a solitary confinement room in a Buddhist temple.

His bad luck did not end there. He met a middle-aged lady Shaman at the mountain. She was preparing food and liquor for a ceremony and prayer. She was possessed by a spirit and was a good fortune teller before she reached middle age. After the ceremony it was custom to share food with everyone. Master Q became a friend of hers and they slept together. It was her intention to have sex with a Chi Gong master to receive Chi energy and shamanic powers. Master Q's Chi energy was almost wiped out. When he visited me in Boston, I was very disappointed about his asthma symptoms and that he had very low Chi energy. He was once a superhuman.

Another friend, Master K, was my Vietnam war comrade. He took Master Q's advice that fasting should be done during a warmer season. He asked a Buddhist temple to rent a solitary confinement room. The temple refused his request because it was for only Buddhist priests who had studied and served in the temple for more than ten years. He tried to bribe them with a large amount of money. They refused to accept it even though the temple needed repairs.

(China has Buddhist and Taoist temples but historically only Buddhist temples can be built in Korea. Buddhism was a national religion and discriminated against other religions. Still Taoism is a temple-less cult as described in the beginning of this book.)

He purchased a small country house and Master Q sealed the doors and windows of the house with boards and nails.

A teenage boy was hired to deliver water and clean excreta. He also watched him 24 hours a day for 21 days. After 15 days Master K got mad and began yelling at them to get out.

When they refused, he tried breaking boards to get out but failed. After 21 days, they let him out, but he was still mad. He gained tremendous power and a sixth sense, but he was possessed by a very strong spirit—so strong no one could exorcise it. Exorcism may only have been possible by Jesus or Shakyamuni Buddha.

We gathered at a restaurant with American students. I spoke to them about our younger days when we could pull a car with teeth. Then, about being under a tire or on our stomach under a car to be run over. Our master had pulled a bus that was loaded with people with his teeth and let the bus run over his stomach.

He challenged me to go out and pull a car with my teeth and be run over after he drank a glass of wine. I told him that we were near 70 years old and that we should stop that nonsense, but he kept on insisting that we should do it. We had a hard time trying to calm him down.

In 1995 or so there was one Korean Tae Kwon Do instructor in the Boston area who tried a demonstration of having a car run over his stomach. Unfortunately, he broke his backbone and damaged both kidneys. An American student donated his kidney to his Tae Kwon Do master.

I think he has passed away. I knew that he had done the demonstration before, but was now over 45 years old. We are able to do it until 35 years old. Unless one is living in a mountain or inside a cave all his life, it should not be attempted. Then, one may possibly be able to do it even around 70 years old age.

It embarrassed me that he became a nymphomaniac. He showed interest in all seminar attending women. It was his part of a possessed spirit. He wore a short T-shirt and thin, summer pants and walked on the street of the small town of Concord during a cold winter day with a temperature of about 20 degrees Fahrenheit. I thought that all the town people thought that an Eskimo had appeared in the town. I begged him to wear decent clothes.

Two of my friends' cases indicate that for a person to become a great man is so difficult. If you are mentally and/or physically stronger than ordinary person, people are often jealous of you. Some people may like you and some people may hate you, too.

Why is it so difficult to become a holy person and/or superman? There are always interventions of an evil spirit who is jealous of your success. It will appear to you just before or after your success. Jesus reached the stage of enlightenment, as Buddha did, after 40 days or 49 days. He faced a temptation from Satan in the New Testament of the Bible. It is probable that there were many more people who tried fasting like Jesus or Buddha in history, but they failed like my two friends.

Ju hwa Ib ma- A martial artist reached the highest goal of Chi gong, but he failed to resist against the temptation of an evil spirit. It does not happen to an external style martial artist. It mostly happens to an internal style martial artist who does it rigorously to build up Chi energy by doing fasting and meditation for weeks. They show tremendous physical power and/or a super sixth sense, but they easily get excited and angry.

Sometimes they do not talk with their own will. An evil spirit makes them talk to a person and the listener will feel annoyed. Another stage is to show much more arrogance and become angry easily.

血

XUE

BLOOD

CHAPTER 8
The Future of Chi Gong

Westerners discovered and adopted the magnetic compass, gun powder, rockets, cooking and the martial arts/physical culture from the Orient long ago. But it is taking a long time for Westerners to begin to accept the metaphysical culture of Chi Gong.

Why? Chi Gong is not tangible, it is impossible to quantify or measure, and the many different styles are confusing to the Western way.

It is a Taoist belief that both chi and spirit are within any object in the universe. We can ask or pray to any object. We can get help or a reply from this object, but only temporarily.

In Asian countries, many people to this day pray to big trees, a big rock or to the mountains. These people can be helped by a shaman who prays to an object or a spirit of the dead. But we should pray only to God our creator, as He is eternal. It is much easier to comprehend any text or religious canon with Chi Gong practice.

From this moment on, politicians throughout the world should practice fasting, Zen meditation and Chi Gong to understand eternal life – then there will be no war.

Muslims make a pilgrimage to Mecca at least once during their life, and many Christians visit Jerusalem. The Indian government is trying to develop the birthplace of Shakyamuni Buddha to create Buddhist tourism, but I do not know if Buddha wants this or if Jesus wants Christians to visit Jerusalem.

Famous Buddhist priests and Taoists wanted to be cremated and have their ashes scattered to nature because they did not want to be worshipped at their grave. It would be the same as seeking fame.

The last pilgrimage for a Taoist or its followers is to travel to the time of the past, present, and future, and any space throughout the universe, without any limitation. How is this accomplished? Through the practice of fasting, Zen, and Chi Gong.

CHAPTER 9
Questions and Answers

1. Why can one person feel more chi energy than another?

One can be born with more or less of a sensitive nature. Usually, women are more sensitive than men and children are more sensitive than adults. Also, it has been reported that one can be trained successfully.

It was reported in a newspaper in the 1960s that a Russian woman could read books with her hand. A modern Western scientist attempted to explain this phenomenon. He surmised that one can be trained to achieve that ability by placing a hand on a piece of black or white paper that is reflected by sunlight. By gradually moving the hand to the black triangle, square or circle on the white paper one may be able to feel the difference of the heat reflected off the paper. It all sounds very scientific, but I prefer to use the following method.

Most children under five years of age have extraordinary senses or a sixth sense. A group of 10 children were given a folded piece of paper with foreign letters written inside. They were asked to hold the paper in the palm of their hand and meditate for a few minutes. After, a Korean TV reporter who was covering the story asked the children to describe what was written on the paper. Most of the children could correctly describe the figures and a few of them even knew how to pronounce the letters. It is commonly believed that we lose the ability to use our sixth sense as we grow older. Once again, it is also more common for women to readily retain the ability better than men. It is common knowledge there are many shamans in Korea. Interestingly, the majority of Korean shamans are women and very few are men. These male shamans are often very feminine in nature.

Once when I was teaching Chi Gong and Zen meditation, I conducted an experiment with my adult class. I gave them each a piece of folded paper which contained drawings of circles, squares, triangles and X's. I asked each of them to hold the folded paper in the palm of their hand and after half an hour of Zen meditation, I asked them to identify the drawing on their folded paper. One person said a circle or ball, another said a square or a rock shaped like a cube and others saw a triangle shape like a roof top. A few people made a mistake or saw nothing at all. One woman said she saw the shape of a horse and I find out later that her paper had an X on it. She came from the Philippines and she had a trace of Spanish ancestry. The "X" in Spanish is pronounced Equis which means a horse! She learned and spoke fluent English (and not Spanish) both in her country and the U.S., but her DNA recognized and retained the Spanish alphabet.

2. Is there a method for attaining chi energy faster?

Yes, there are several methods, but beware of the hidden dangers:

    a. Regular Chi Gong practice that is shown in this book.
    b. Fasting with the guidance of a good master.
    c. You may quickly glance at the sun while most of your eyes are covered with your fingers. Special breathing is required. Sometimes permanent eye damage can occur even while attaining greater chi energy.
    d. Chinese herbal tablets with cinnabar (derived from mercury). After taking it on is able to get rid of the poison in the body through the skin's pores. It is said to guarantee longevity and eternal youth. However, five emperors died following this teaching of a Taoist master during the Tang Dynasty in China. (618-907 A.D.)

3. How is it possible to prevent altitude sickness and the deep-sea diving sickness?

At the end of Chapter 3, there is a breathing technique as follows:
> *Slowly inhale, hold, exhale and hold. Just after inhaling, immerse your body in a swimming pool and hold a fixed object and come out while practicing one cycle of breathing. Repeat and gradually a person may dive deeper every few days. One needs a good master for this method. This is one of the Ninja training methods.*

Sue, who is mentioned in the introduction of this book, sent Chi energy to her boyfriend in Ireland from her home in Cambridge, Massachusetts. She received a call from him the next day. Later, she then traveled to Tibet just after the first edition of my book was published in 1999. In Tibet, because of the altitude sickness, it is a common practice for visitors to rent oxygen tanks from hotels, but Sue did not feel it necessary. She saw a Japanese tourist choke and collapse just prior to using the oxygen tank. After her experience, a few people came to me for instruction before traveling to Tibet. After studying and practicing this breathing technique, this group of people had no difficulty breathing and did not rent oxygen tanks.

4. Where have all the Chi Gong masters gone?

A Chi Gong master came from a distant high mountain and decided to take a young man from the village and return to the mountain and make him his student. Both meditated and fasted in a cave for more than a year. It was very quiet and isolated from the outside world. The young student learned and observed the amazing ability of his master. His master could move a small object with a glance and could look through his body to diagnose disease. Also, he could heal sickness in animals, birds, reptiles and even trees and plants.

After a time, the young man came down from the mountain to show off what he learned from the master. The village people were very excited to meet the master and he healed most of the diseases in the village. Soon after, the student and master moved to a small town, where he treated more people and made more money. One day the master complained that he did not like sleeping in a small inn. So, the student moved the master into a nice hotel in a nearby big city. He and his business became even more successful. Later, he complained, again, that he wanted expensive clothes and wanted to see a nice-looking woman, too. Soon after, people began to complain that the master did not have the ability to heal and was no better than the local Reiki healer.

There have been many similar stories over the years. Some masters come from China, Korea, and Japan. As mentioned in a story earlier in the book, if one becomes overly involved with business, it is likely that God will take away their ability to heal. Jesus, Buddha, yogis, and Chi Gong masters retain the healing powers of those who did not become greedy over the power of healing.

5. Are there still many hermits and Taoists in the mountains of Korea as described in the beginning of Chapter 1?

Yes, there are many hermits, run-away criminals, and spies from North and South Korea. In addition, shamans occasionally visit these areas to fast and pray for guidance from spirits or to be possessed by them. Most shamans are female; they often bring food such as meat, fish or fruit for ceremonial purposes.

When shamans pray, they first wash their bodies with cold water from a woodland stream, and they often perform the ceremonies naked. They usually pray and fast for 21 or in some cases, 100 days. This can be dangerous because sometimes they are attacked or murdered by criminals.

6. Why are there so many Chi Gong styles and why are they taught so differently?

As with yoga, Kung Fu, martial arts, and acupuncture, Chi Gong is a very old practice and has developed in many ways. Chi Gong has a history of more than a thousand years. You can study any style because the main principles and purposes are the same, that is, to:

1. Open Chi stagnation
2. Build up Chi energy
3. Circulate Chi energy
4. Maintain Chi circulation

7. Do you teach or run a Chi Gong camp?

I mainly teach private lessons and will often teach a seminar on weekends. Occasionally, I teach a weekend Chi Gong camp. I plan to teach more camps in the near future.

Check for details on my web site www.kwangmooryu.com

Taking Shoes Off at Home

You must take off shoes in your home.

I have observed the American lifestyle for the last 40 years from the point of view of medical anthropology. Americans contract more lung cancer than Asians, even though Americans smoke less. Also, sanitation and medical facilities are much better in Asian countries and pollution control is better than in most of the third world countries.

What is big difference between East and West? Koreans, Japanese and Indians take off their shoes at home. But most Americans wear shoes in the house.

When Americans come home from work, they usually take a shower or wash their hands. They also use air purifiers, humidifiers, heaters and air conditioners to control the air quality. Furthermore, they wash and disinfect mattresses and pillows for allergens. But germs are spread all over the floor from shoes that were worn all day and traveled many different places.

Even if one vacuums several times per week, it does not disinfect floors completely. If an infant plays or crawls around, they could contact germs dropped from the shoes of family and guests.

Also, almost every household has one, two or even three pets. Are they kept clean and sanitized conditions?

Taking Shoes Off at Home

Most Asians, especially Koreans and Japanese, dry their bodies and feet thoroughly after taking a shower. Most Caucasian Americans do not dry their body and feet enough with a towel and then step on the bathroom floor. The bathmat gets wet and usually they do not wash it and leave it there for days. It will produce many germs as in a medical lab incubator.

For another example, if an electrician or cable TV repairman enters the home, there can be more than ten different germs from under the ground that can be tracked inside. This can affect toddlers who may pick up toys or snacks from the floor.

A physician may allow a patient to wear shoes while lying down on the exam table. Germs can be transmitted easily to the body because it is close to the wounds, mouth and nose. Americans even sit on a bed or lie down while wearing shoes.

How often are your hands washed and shoes cleaned? When an electrician or cable television repairman visits your house, give them house shoes or covers to wear temporarily while inside your home.

Fig. X-1: *Cavemen wore shoes inside the cave*

Fig. X-2: *Modern day families wear shoes inside the home*

Preventing and Treating COVID-19 Through Chi Gong

SWEAT IT OUT!

To adequately treat infections a basic understanding of how the body works to rid itself of harmful organisms is important. During the germ infection, having a fever is not a bad thing; it is our body's natural defense mechanism kicking in to fight against harmful bacteria, viruses, and other invading organisms. Modern scientific research reveals that germs (bacteria and viruses) are only able to live in our body when the body is at a normal temperature level.

The traditional Korean method of healing the body against bacterial or viral infections is through elevating the body temperature during the beginning of an infection.

It does not have to be a respiratory organ infection only, even you can apply it to any infection such as tonsillitis, infected wounds with mild fever, etc.

When you catch a cold or flu (bacteria and virus), first check the body temperature. (97-degree F /36.1 C- normal).

It is advised that the person heat up the room. This can be done by using a portable electric heater and humidifier. Prior to the procedure you may take a hot shower or bath. Then cover your face with a bath towel and /or wear hooded sweatshirt and socks. Cover your entire body with two blankets. Place one stick on each side of the armpits to make breathing easier – for example, make a tent for breathing when you have a towel over the face. The sticks should be one inch in diameter (2.5 cm) and 20 inches (50 cm) long or longer for bigger person. Then you will sweat it out for an hour. This process can be safely repeated for two or three days until symptom have improved. Your body temperature will go up to 2-degree F/ 1.1 degree C after an hour of sweating.

For this to be affective you must start at the first sign of symptoms; when you start feeling like you are coming down with the common cold, a scratchy throat but virus infection symptoms are mild fever (98.6-degree F/ 37 C), chills, ache, fatigue, cough, and headache.

For example, then you must sweat it out immediately and not wait. You may feel much better, repeat it next day but keep in mind that even if you feel better this does not mean it is completely gone. You need to this process for two or three more days until all symptoms are better.

Who can and cannot use this method?
Do not start this procedure, when you start coughing up phlegm, vomiting, shortness of breath, chest pain and have high fever (over 101 degree / 38.3 C to 106-degree F/ 41.1 degree C). You must go to emergency room or seek for urgent medical care.

One can do this procedure in a private sauna as well. Wear a hooded sweatshirt, trousers, and socks. Heat the room to a temperature of 150 degrees F (66 degree C). Do this for 30 minutes.

After sweating it out. One should drink enough water to prevent dehydration. When a person has been infected by the Corona Virus, the first three days of symptoms are usually very mild. During this time the amount of the virus is at its lowest level in the body, therefore sweating it out at the beginning is the best method to rid the body of the virus.

I have been treating hundreds of patients with sweat it out method for common cold and flu symptoms in Boston, Massachusetts for twenty years and ten years in Oklahoma City.

There have been many individuals and many families in Oklahoma City area who got better through using the sweat it out method during the initial stage of their corona virus infection. Doing the sweat-out method sooner was the best thing. They did not suffer symptoms at all in the most of cases.

Last June, a mother whose son was thirty years old and who is naturopathic doctor with a practice in Colorado informed me that her son had used this method.

He became infected by corona virus and using his sauna was able to sweat it out and able to rid himself of the virus through this. He did not get this information from me. I am guessing that he obtained this information of sweating it out from another source.

This method may apply to any infectious disease, infection of the eye, ears, throat infections such as tonsillitis and sinus infections. It can be used in infections on the internal organs provided there is no high fever (over 100-degree F.) You can apply this method to any type of infectious disease and be able to see results.

We are in the age of uncertainty of what kind of virus will be spread and developed. The vaccine may not work well or mutate as often as the influenza virus. The time is now, and until we need a permanent solution to cure coronavirus, "sweat it out".

Preventing and Treating COVID-19   205

If there is no cure for coronavirus, then Western medical practitioners might potentially resort to experimenting on coronavirus with mice, cats, dogs, monkeys, and humans in a medical trial by using elevated body temperature method. We knew that germ live in our body temperature level. We can get rid of it by elevate body temperature. Is it possible to cooling down our body below our normal body temperature level to get rid of it? I guessed and imagined it for long time.

I found out that very young infants, the elderly cannot reach high fevers during a germ-related or viral infection, because their bodies are weak. Their body temperatures are unable to elevate to a fever level. The physical response of infants and elderly bodies appear to cool down instead of raising to a fever level.

I have not confirmed this theory on lower body temperatures of infants and the elderly from Western medical science yet. If anyone researches the correlation of lower body temperatures, then potentially the coronavirus or germ can be cured. I would like to suggest that any scientist should research on this subject.

I have treated many covid 19 patients who have had coughing, headache, loss of sense and smell, permanent lung damage, heart issues, liver issues, and gallbladder issues. I helped these people successfully except few senior citizens who are over 80 years old.

EPILOGUE

I published a book, *Oriental Medicine and Cancer*, in 1996 which was a sequel to the book, *Acupuncture for Self-Defense*, published in 1971 (it is now out of print but will be revised soon). *Oriental Medicine and Cancer* 1998 published book deals with the causative factors of cancer from the Oriental medical viewpoint. Namely, this view holds that surgery scars and physical injuries block chi flow in the acupuncture channel and cause cancer, as if attacking a pressure (acupuncture) point in martial arts to paralyze an opponent.

In the Far East, the license for acupuncture requires a minimum of 4-6 years of college and the passing of a national license exam in China, Korea, or Japan. The practice of both eastern and western medicines requires schooling and passing license exams in both fields. In the U.S., to obtain a license you need a 4-year college degree with an internship.

Oriental medicine is an art form, as is martial arts. All marital artists do not have the same ability. Some, like beginners, wear white belts; the experts wear black belts. Some masters' abilities are beyond a belt system.

Never judge Oriental Medicine by one visit to an acupuncturist or herbalist, especially in the U.S. Many who call themselves an acupuncturist do not know how to give chi energy through the needle. I believe when the original form of acupuncture migrated from India to China, the essential part of Oriental Medicine was how to give chi or move chi energy stagnation in our body through the needle. Where modern research on Oriental Medicine should begin is with chi energy flow in the human body.

A YouTube video shows an American man who claims to be a Ghostbuster with a video camera. He seems to like to eat beef steak and hamburger. I like to suggest to him that he should be on a vegetable diet and practice fasting one day per week for a few months. Then, he might feel some spirit. It is easier to feel a bad spirit than a holy spirit.

Chi Gong centers have many small branches all over the U.S. and other countries. Once it had more fame, but now this organization has declined in size due to bad scandals. The biggest problem is the leader - a Korean guy who never had martial art experience nor Chi Gong experience, he just learned it from someone for few months and then he organized it like a cult. He does not even know the basic principles of the nature of Internal and External Martial Art. As I mentioned in the beginning of the book, Chi Gong should be focused on breathing exercises, meditation and Tai Chi or Bagua movements. Nevertheless, he instructed a student with heavy weight training included. Eventually the person became exhausted and a heart attack. She died during heavy exercise with heavy weight training. I am in a situation of teaching both internal and external styles. So, I want to make mentioned of the kind of caution one should take.

The Chinese government does not like people gathering except for the communist party, not even religious gatherings. They even oppressed the Chi Gong group. A Chinese man who wrote or translated many Chinese martial art books including a Qi Gong book. He learned Chinese martial art at around 30 years old in age while in America. He graduated college in the U.S. and was good at English. He, his student and a politician try to regulate the licensing of Qi Gong teaching in America. America is a democratic country. They will be suffering from consequences of arrogant attitude towards Qi Cong (Chi Gong).

A Korean Tae Kwon Do instructor claimed to be a master. He passed away last year. He acted the same as the Chinese man. He graduated from a college in America and learned Tae Kwon Do from my friend in America around the age of 30. He also published a Tae Kwon Do book. His last words were, "I learned Tae Kwon Do in Korea when I was teenager."

I do not smell of any sweat, blood, or tears from these books, but I do have a little smell of deodorant.

I want to repeat again that if you want to learn Chi Gong correctly, you must find a reputable master. If you want to learn or teach Chi Gong; first clean up your soul by quit smoking cigarettes and doing marijuana, alcohol, or recreational drugs. Do more meditation, eat a vegetarian diet and fast intermittently. One day you should achieve the ability to do simple exorcism. You have to have strong willpower and evil spirits will be scared of you.

If you just teach without enough knowledge of Chi Gong, one day all your Chi will be wiped out and you will get old faster. It will shorten your life.

GLOSSARY

1. **Ai Ki Do** – Japanese form of self-defense, similar to Hap Ki Do.

2. **Asi point** - any point on the skin where finger pressure may cause pain other than the common acupuncture points.

3. **Ba Gua** -- an internal style of Chinese marital arts, similar to Tai Chi but with an emphasis on palm techniques.

4. **Buddhist** – One who believes and follows the teachings of Shakyamuni Buddha. Buddha,4which means the "Awakened One" taught that through spiritual training, one can break free of illusion and karmic consequences and become enlightened.

5. **Cha Ryuk** – Korean form of martial art Chi Gong.

6. **Chi** – the body's internal energy, an electro-magnetic wave force

7. **Chi Gong** – method of Chi energy cultivating exercise which includes Zen meditation, fasting, and breathing exercises.

8. **Dan Gun** – the first king of Korea who ruled approximately 5,000 years ago.

9. **Feng Shui** – the ancient Chinese art of geomancy, which enables us to decide how and where to build a house or arrange a room so that we live in harmony with our surroundings.

10. **Hap Ki Do** – Korean art of self-defense which utilizes kicking, punching, throwing, and joint-locking techniques.

11. **Judo** – An Olympic sport, developed in Japan. Judo is a form of self-defense that is similar to American wrestling.

12. **Karate** – Japanese form of self-defense.

13. **Kung Fu** – Chinese form of martial arts.

14. **Lama** – a Buddhist priest of Tibet.

15. **Sa Myung Dang** – one of Suhsan's disciples and Successor

16. **Sanskrit** – Classical old Hindu language which originated in India in the 4th Century.

17. **Shakyamuni Buddha** – the founder of the Buddhist religion, who lived about 2,500 years ago in India.

18. **Shaolin Temple** – a 1,500 years-old Buddhist temple in China, located in the Song Mountain, Hunan Province, famous for Zen meditation and Chinese marital arts.

19. **Suhsan** – literally means West Mountain. A Korean Buddhist priest (A.D. 1554 to 1610) who lived during Yi Cho Sun dynasty. He is famous for organizing the Buddhist military against the Japanese invasion. Legend has it that while he was in Japan after the war, negotiating the return of Korean prisoners, the Japanese tried to kill him while he was sleeping. They pretended to add firewood to the fire in his room to warm it up, but actually intended to set fire to this room. When they returned the next morning, rather than charred remains, they discovered that the room was covered in white frost.

20. **Tae Kwon Do** – Korean art of self-defense.

21. **Tai Chi** – one type of the inner style Chinese Martial Arts form, which cultivates chi energy through slow movements and focused breathing exercises, rather than concentrating on building muscle strength.

22. **Tai San** – a mountain in San Tung province in China. It is well known for its beautiful scenery and many Taoist temples. Many emperors worshipped there throughout history, including Emperor Chin, who built the great wall.

23. **Tan Tien** – also pronounced Dan Tien, it is the center of energy, located one inch below the navel.

24. **Taoist** – one who believes in and follows the Taoist philosophy.

25. **Xing Yi** – an internal style of Chinese marital arts, similar to Tai Chi but with an emphasis on using the fist.

INDEX

A
Acupuncture......19,30,87,95,102,116,117,118,120,182,184, 185,206
ADD... 28
Aikido..25
Allah...61
Ameipa 18, 64
Asthma...65, 187

B
Ba Gua...23
Bends 112
Bodhidharma...25, 78
Breach Delivery 95
Buddha....................19,20,27,31,49,56,61,62,63,70,137,139, 188,189,191,196
Buddhism 25, 187

C
Cancer 61, 65, 106
Celibate 73, 143
Cesarean Delivery.. 95
Cha Ryuk 23, 24, 142, 200
Chanting..............................23, 60, 61, 62, 63, 143
Chi..19
Chi Gong...15,16,17,18,40,42,46,47,48,50,56,57,60,61,62,68, 74,75,81,82,84,86,95,106,108,110,114,120,136,137,138,141,1 42,146,147,177,178,179,182,183,184,187,191,193,194,197,20 6,207,208
Christian...62, 70, 140, 191
Cremate...192

D
Dan Gun 18, 63, 210
Dehydration 64, 203
Diabetic 65, 97, 100
Digestive enzyme.. 77

Index

DU#20 .... 61, 160, 172

F
Fasting 18,19,23,63,64,65,66,67,68,140,186,189,192
Feng Shui .... .57

G
Glossolalia 62

H
Hap Ki Do 23, 25
Hibernation 69
Hindus 69
Holy Spirit 61, 62, 207

J
Jerusalem 191
Jesus 19,61,62,70,137,140,143,182,184,188,189,191,196
Judo 23, 25, 136

K
Karate 23, 25, 28, 136, 177
Kidney failure 65, 141
Kung Fu ....,,,,,,,23, 28, 141, 197

L
Lama 17
Levitate 106
Lhasa 142

M
Mecca 191
Mental illness 65
Miscarriage 95
Mohammed 61, 63, 70
Moses .... ,61, 63, 70, 137, 143

N
Nirvana 27, 68, 69

O
Old Testament..63, 70

P
Parasite..65, 67
Praying 23, 70, 73, 143
Pregnant 32, 95
Psychic 63, 136

R
Rehabilitation..101, 109

S
Shakyamuni Buddha..........19,25,27,31,49,70,139,188,191
Sanskrit..21, 27
Satan...63, 140, 182, 189
Shaman.........................18,62,63,70,187,191,193,196
Shaolin Temple...25
Simmani...73
Sinai, Mount..63

T
Tae Kwon Do................23,24,25,28,117,136,188,207,208
Tai Chi..........................18,23,27,28,63,177,178,179,207
Tai San..17
Tan Tien......................18,36,37,46,48,56,61,62,125,182
Tang Dynasty 56, 194
Taoist...16,17,18,19,30,31,37,44,49,57,58,63,64,69,70,71,74, 101,106,115,141,143,179,183,191,192,194,196

U
Ulcerative colitis 65

X
Xing Yi 23

Y
Yogi 16,18,57,63,69,70,78,137,138,139,179,196

Z
Zen meditation...18,23,24,25,26,27,28,30,45,49,59,60,68,69, 141,182,191,194

Eastern culture and Western culture

When I arrived in America in 1970, I saw an evangelist on TV criticize meditation as "a hippie's demonic ceremony". Meditate on what? Meditate on not thinking. Meditate on clear thought. Meditation is not familiar with American culture. Over fifty years has passed. Meditation, or Zen meditation, is practiced everywhere--in Yoga class, Martial arts schools, psychiatrist offices, and even at some Christian churches.

In my Kinesiology book, Americans can easily and clearly understand all the photos with instructions.
My Chi Gong book describes the invisible power of Chi energy. Chi energy is not tangible, so some people can feel chi energy, and some people cannot feel chi energy; other people interpret chi energy as a false claim. Many people can only understand worldly phenomena through tangible senses only. "Seeing is Believing".

Acupuncture treatment is popular among Americans. More than thirty-five percent of Americans have been treated with Acupuncture. Acupuncture theory is based on following the Acupuncture Chi energy channels. Western nerve system is tangible and visible, but Acupuncture channels are invisible.

Martial Arts in America

The most participated sport in America is neither baseball, basketball nor football. Asian martial arts are the most "participated in" popular sport in America. Americans understand punches, kicks, grappling, and throwing well. However, many Americans struggle to interpret pattern forms such as Kata.

For correct martial arts forms and patterns, check out my Kinesiology book and other books on Amazon.com.

Kinesiology videos are on **www.kwangmooryu.com** with examples of correct and incorrect form interpretations.

Since most Americans perceive form patterns as very difficult to perform easily, and since most Americans are not familiar with the Korean culture, martial arts is beneficial as a practical application on how to apply correct kinesiology to daily working activities.

I have treated ADHD students with simple forms. If the student progresses, I gradually use more advanced forms as moving meditations.

THE ULTIMATE GUIDE THAT WILL HELP YOU TOWARDS BODY EFFICIENCY AND PREVENT INJURIES

KINESIOLOGY
COMMON SENSE

Myung Chill Kim

Master Kim's long awaited book detailing the kinesiology of Martial Arts

INCLUDES 320 PHOTOS

1. Shoveling
2. Sledge Hammering
3. Chopping Wood
4. How to Lift Up Patient
5. Lifting Boxes
6. Opening Jars
7. Pulling Teeth
8. Cleaver/Butcher's Knife
9. Post Office
10. Handling Library Books
11. Fire Rescue
12. Cowboy
13. Pushing Car
14. Baseball Pitching
15. Baseball Batting
16. Softball Pitching
17. Throwing Football
18. Basketball
19. Tennis
20. Golf
21. Frisbee
22. Javelin
23. Discus
24. Shot Put
25. Bowling
26. Judo
27. Hand Grenade
28. Police Baton
29. Knife Throwing
30. Axe Throwing
31. Lance
32. German Sword
33. Pistol
34. Bayonet Skill

WATCH KINESIOLOGY VIDEO DEMO AT
www.kwangmooryu.com

6" x 9"
300 Pages
$9.95 USD

KINESIOLOGY: COMMON SENSE

EXCERPT

Standing and walking homo sapiens, or early modern humans, appeared on earth nearly 2 million years ago. The first humans began to use hands and tools for farming, built houses, hunted animals, and were skilled at warfare. Except for a few martial arts experts in India, China, and Korea, the first humans did not know how to use tools properly. Using tools with the correct kinesiology not only prevents injuries, but also helps the body with "energy efficiency".

Using correct kinesiology will foster productivity. For example, if one uses a computer mouse and feels numbness on the hand, then try moving the hand to the center of the keyboard. Another option is to replace using a mouse at a desktop with a laptop touch pad. You will feel much better at once.

If the 20th century was the age of globalization, then 21st century will be space travel age. Please read this book before migrating to another planet.

Shoveling, sledge hammering, cutting meat, breaking roof tiles, and demonstrating correct martial art techniques are some of the free videos you can watch on my website listed above. This book, "Kinesiology: Common Sense", shows the reader how to apply the correct kinesiology using both hands, the waist, and sequential stomping.

Using the correct kinesiology will at first appear to be more graceful, like ballet. The benefits of using correct kinesiology result in two to three times more force and power. Also, using the correct kinesiology prevents injuries.

The correct kinesiology methods prescribed in this book come from ancient martial art techniques used for thousands of years, passed down many generations only through elite martial arts warriors. Refer also to my other book, Myung Chill Kim's Tae Kwon Do (Kinesiology of martial arts) (Kwang Moo Ryu Style), also available on www.amazon.com

Check out
www.youtube.com/@myungchillkim and
www.kwangmooryu.com

Tae Kwon Do

Kwang Moo Ryu Style
Kinesiology of Martial Arts

Volume I: Essentials

Fifth Revision

Myung Chill Kim

Kinesiology for Martial Artists and Athletes of the 21st Century

The study of Kinesiology does not align with martial arts movements modernized over the last 100 years.

Master Myung Chill Kim has combined theories of Tae Kwon Do, Karate, Shaolin and Praying Mantis style Kung Fu and Boxing to:

- Correct the profound loss of historical peak efficiency, with CHANGE which must come to the Basics, Forms, Breaking, Sparring and Fighting Techniques.
- Learn how to paralyze an opponent with Praying Mantis and Kicking techniques.
- Learn how to practice with a patented Isokinetic Resistance Pad.
- Reveal the secret of Maximum force using ankle and wrist weights to rebalance and strengthen the form's dynamics.
- Cast the VIBRATING PALM (Iron Palm) with this training method.

8.5" x 11" 300 pages, 353 illustrations
Visit www.TKDBOOK.COM for more information

Myung Chill Kim
1965 - Korean Tiger Troops TKD instructor (Vietnam War)
1981 - Criminal Investigator for New York City Dept. of Ports.
1986 – Degree of Doctor of Oriental Medicine

Author of:
1971 - "Acupuncture for Self Defense"
1997 - "Oriental Medicine and Cancer"
1999 - "Chi Gong: Medicine from God"
2009 - "Tae Kwon Do (Kwang Moo Ryu)"

$39.95
ISBN 978-0-9970399-7-9

Books are available for purchase on amazon.com

ALSO AVAILABLE IN
GERMAN LANGUAGE
ON AMAZON.COM

5th Edition Available on Spring 2023

EXCERPT:

If someone teaches ballet, the movement is standard all over the world. However, Tae Kwon Do kicks are done differently by each person. **We need a standard movement with kinesiology.**

What is the correct side kick? What is the standard side kick?

A side kick should have both arms moving in opposite directions during the kick. This correct side kick posture results in the most powerful side kick, plus if the opponent is blocking or pushing, the side kick posture balance will be sustained with proper kinesiology.

Sidekicks with Tae Kwon Do and Karate use two hands holding in front of the chest while kicking. Some martial artists incorrectly think two hands held onto the chest pose is better than both hands stretching sideways, as in the figure below. Unfortunately, the hands can only be used to punch after the foot lands on the ground.

From the kicking pose, bring hands together, land the foot first, then punch. Whether the hands are stretched or together while kicking does not make a big difference.

These photos are in the Tae Kwon Do book. You can see the Tae Kwon Do videos on www.kwangmooryu.com. If you want to learn the correct way of martial arts, subscribe to my Kwang Moo Ryu videos.

225

Above is an incorrect jumping sidekick in most Tae Kwon Do and Karate textbooks. This kick looks like an airplane with two wings on one side. Even when you kick the air, even when you hit the target, or especially when the opponent blocks you, you will have a crash landing on the ground.

Above is the correct jumping side kick.

This perfect balance of the jumping side kick kinesiology using the right hand and left-hand balance pushing in opposite directions, is correct.
This is the correct position for the jumping side kick, even when you kick the air, even when you hit the target, or even when the opponent blocks you, you can have a safe landing.

Roundhouse kick
www.kwangmooryu.com

The correct kinesiology for the roundhouse kick technique is as follows: swing arms and turn the waist before the kick to create two to three times more powerful force than the ordinary Tae Kwon Do or Karate kick. This kinesiology technique also prevents injuries.

Watch accuracy of martial art movements
www.kwangmooryu.com
The watermelon video on YouTube is different than in the photo.

The watermelon in the video has a spear holding the round, very hard watermelon that resembles a basketball. Master Kim was able to slice the watermelon one inch from the spearhead.

Master Kim is demonstrating speed and accuracy by cutting a watermelon with a razor-sharp samurai sword on a student's stomach with his eyes closed.

Without the sense of sight, Master Kim can conquer the sixth sense of slicing a watermelon with no sight.

The watermelon depicted above is a hard, round watermelon that was available in the late fall season in Boston, Massachusetts.

Please watch my health and Martial Art demonstration videos on my channels at **www.kwangmooryu.com**.

I have twenty-one videos, but I have finished uploading only nine videos on my website.

The videos contain twenty-one correct Tae Kwon Do forms (Japanese call this form *kata*).

Most of the "breaking demonstration" movements, even using a stationary object, are incorrect in both form and style. See the Tae Kwon Do textbook.

Forms

Tae Kwon Do and Karate practitioners are good in sparring, but the forms (*kata*) do not have much connected movements. If they are engaged in real fighting situations, they can fight as they are practicing sparring in a school. But if they were to be sucker punched or kicked first, they would be at a major disadvantage.

Kung Fu forms have more connected movements than Tae Kwon Do and Karate forms, but there are not enough sparring techniques for it to be useful in real situations.

Shadow Boxing movements are very useful in real fighting situations, even if you suddenly get hit first by an opponent and you can still use continuous movements.

Most of Kwang Moo Ru's forms were designed for continuous movement in practical applications. It has the best martial arts forms for the 21st century with correct kinesiology and connected movements.

Bruce Lee passed away in 1973. He learned Tae Kwon Do kicks from a Korean master in Oklahoma City, Oklahoma, and from another master in Washington D.C. around the late 1960's. Unfortunately, Lee's masters were unable to teach him the correct kinesiology of kicking.

Lee practiced Tae Kwon Do kicks for many hours per day, including roundhouse and back spinning kick combinations. He injured his lower back and had spinal surgery. The surgeon advised Lee that he should not practice any more kicks for the rest of his life. Once Lee reached to gain world famous status, many movie roles were rushed onto him. When Lee shot movies in Asia, he used a Korean Tae Kwon Do black belt as his double because he had too much pain and had to use steroids and endo-opioids to ease back pain.

Therefore, non-kinesiology-based movements of hands and feet maneuvers will injure martial artists and shorten their lifespans. Survey shows that the average life span of martial artists are 70 years of age.

The correct application of kinesiology in martial arts to scenes of UFC full contact matches might be changed. However, because Master Kim's martial art techniques are very powerful and dangerous, he is concerned that these techniques will permanently injure or kill the opponents, even in UFC fighting sports arenas.

Real martial artists cannot play with these serious techniques. If martial artists apply this kinesiology of Martial Art techniques, then more serious injuries will occur.

THE LAST 120 YEARS HAS BEEN THE DARK AGES OF MARTIAL ARTS. WE SHOULD PRACTICE CORRECT KINESIOLOGY FOR PRESENT AND FUTURE GENERATIONS.

跆拳道

TAE   KWON   DO

ORIENTAL MEDICINE AND CANCER

Revised Edition

MYUNG CHILL KIM

REVISED EDITION OF THE GROUNDBREAKING 1996 BOOK WITH NEWLY DEVELOPED TREATMENT METHODS

Over 50% of women have hip and back problems

Many cancers result from **physical injury** and **surgical scars** which block the flow of Chi energy in the body.

It is not a coincidence that a patient with hip joint problems may develop breast, ovarian, testicular or prostate cancer on the same side. In addition, they may also develop vertigo, reproductive organ prolapse and Parkinson's Disease.

Problems on one side of the body can affect other areas on the same side:
- 4th Toe <---------> 4th Finger
- Ankle <---------> Wrist
- Knee joint <---------> Elbow joint
- Hip joint <---------> Shoulder joint

○ *Revised Edition* introduces Master Kim's revolutionary **Diagonal Symmetry Points Technique**

○ Learn how to make easy and precise diagnoses and prognoses with your fingertips

○ Hundreds of illustrations and photos

▶ For helpful videos, please visit www.youtube.com/@myungchillkim

7" x 10"
344 Pages
$29.95 USD

E-book available for the first time on amazon.com

235

Traditional acupuncture books and teachings at acupuncture schools has been emphasizing mainly internal organ problems caused by lack of sanitation, malnutrition, parasitic infestation, and infectious disease.

However, acupuncturists who face the modern Westernized world do not commonly see the above listed problems because medical providers, clinics, hospitals and pharmacies in the Western world can cure many of these issues.

Modern Western society has more muscular skeletal problems caused by car accidents, sports injuries, surgery scars, etc.

Oriental Medicine and Cancer is the first acupuncture book that deals with muscular skeletal problems pertaining to Western society today.

This book is the first time in acupuncture history that addresses how to deal with Western modernized issues.

Introduction:

"Gentlemen and Ladies."
"I have traveled around the eastern, western, southern, and northern parts of the United States."

To understand Oriental Medicine, Westerners must open their minds to the vast differences between Eastern and Western ways of thinking. There are profound differences in orientation, approaches to movement, ways in which language is used to refer to movement in nature, and the perception of how human beings are related to nature.

People in American, European, Arabic, and Indian cultures think about direction in the following sequence: North, South, East, and West (four directions). Western culture is characterized by movement and exploration.

The sailing of ships in search of new lands and new opportunities for trade, and the voyages through space in pursuit of knowledge about the universe — these restless movements of the Western mind are perhaps guided using the Northern star as a point of orientation. In Taoist terms, we would say that as a culture of movement, the West is Yang.

In Eastern culture, in contrast, Chinese and Korean people orient according to: East, West, South, and North. People have been tempered by thousands of years of agriculture. The orientation towards life and health is based on farming, literally cultivating "what is." Relative to the West, we could be called a Yin culture. When Koreans sleep, they point their heads towards the East or South. As you will learn in this book, Chi Gong and other forms of meditation also recommend facing East and South. The rising of the sun and its heating of the earth influenced the livelihood of our ancestors so much that we still use it as a basis for orienting our lives.

The Chinese, Mongols, and Tibetans have basic directional orientations that they use in daily living. In China, the dead are displayed in their houses during mourning in coffins with their heads facing north or the deceased is buried facing north underground; this tradition has been adopted by Koreans. Mongols, like Koreans, build their houses facing South to take advantage of the sun's light and heat since their weather can be extremely cold.

Another example illustrating the differences in orientation between the West and the East is the compass.

The Chinese originally invented the magnetic compass, called the Chi Nan Jen - Chi meaning pointing; Nan meaning South and Jen meaning needle. Westerns assumed, when they recreated the compass for their use, that the magnetic direction was north. Once again, we see the clear-cut difference in orientation.

I specialize in treating breast tumors with Chi energy. After the first treatment, you will get surprising results.

I treat pregnant women with chi infusion with or without needles once or twice per month. After the pregnant women delivers her baby, she will recover much faster and her baby will be born with extra chi energy and will be more energetic than other babies. The American government has spent over 50 billion dollars for cancer research since the 1970s Nixon Administration, yet still has not found the cure for many cancers.

I treat people with acupuncture needle with Chi energy infusion. .

Westerners think pollution affects organs inside of body from cancer-causing pollutants only. This is a great misconception is Western medicine's black and white thinking concepts.

Yin Yang Theory means different forces opposite of each other that coexist.

Example: Internal and External.

Cancer is caused by external injuries that block the chi flow channels too.

Example: Spinal injuries and surgery scars can cause cancer.

Athletes can get Chi energy from me and their athletic performance will improve and may break world record

Even after one treatment, you may feel lighter and more energetic.
info@myungchillkim.com

Fig. 6 - 5
"BA GUA"

Who designed the original Ba Gua symbol?
How long ago? No one knows.
In China, the Chinese interpret Ba Gua symbol as Two-Dimensional.
North, South, East, West,
Northeast, Northwest, Southeast, Southwest (8 directions).

I am the first person in thousands of years who interprets Ba Gua as three-dimensional.

I am also the first author who understood the original mind of the Ba Gua creator. My book has the Western Cartesian Coordination Sytem in Eastern Yin/Yang

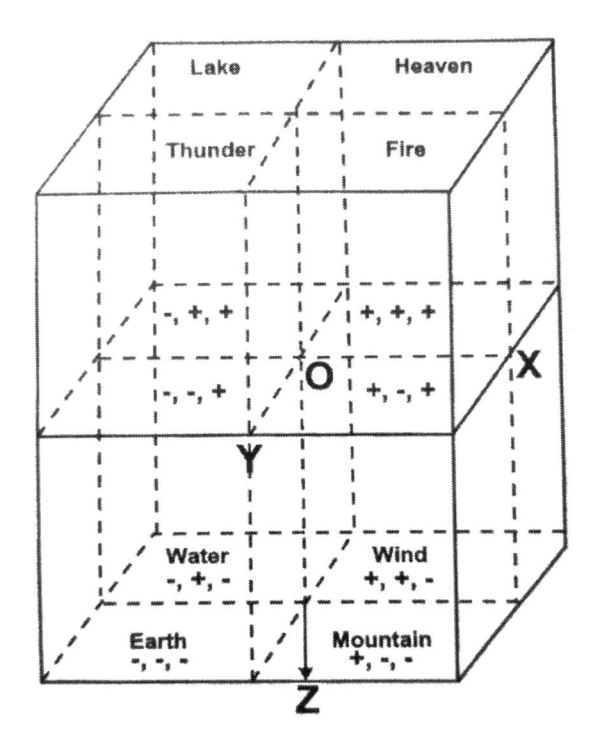

Three Dimension

Fig. 6-11

The three-dimensional Ba Gua system depicted on Fig. 6-10 becomes this photo, Fig. 6-11. Ba Gua can be applied to a building with second story and eight rooms. Four downstairs rooms, four up stair rooms stair rooms.

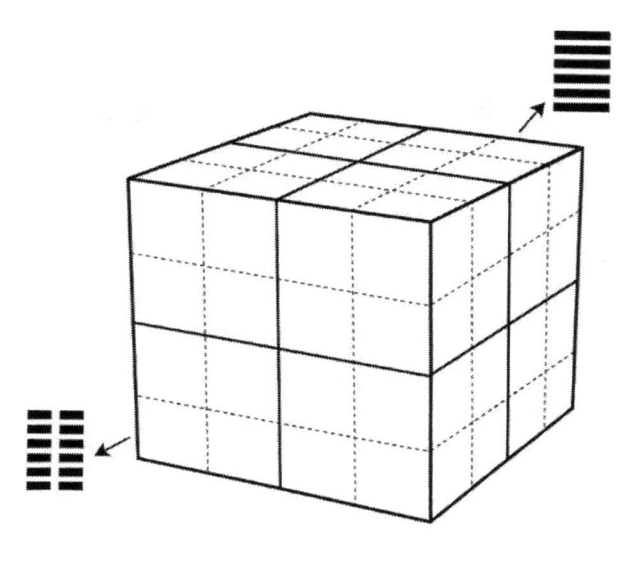

Fig. 6-12

    This is a famous I-Ching system is usually used for fortune-telling, using a six-hexagram system. I converted this I-Ching system as a four-story building wit with sixty-four rooms. Each room of the original eight room building is divided eight, leaving sixty-four rooms. I was the best mathematician in my class as a young scholar.

Books are available for purchase on amazon.com

EACH MONTH, I WILL PUT
a Martial Arts Newsletter
WITH AN ARTICLE AND
PHOTO AND/OR VIDEO
FOR FREE ONLY AT

WWW.KWANGMOORYU.COM

TAI CHI YU

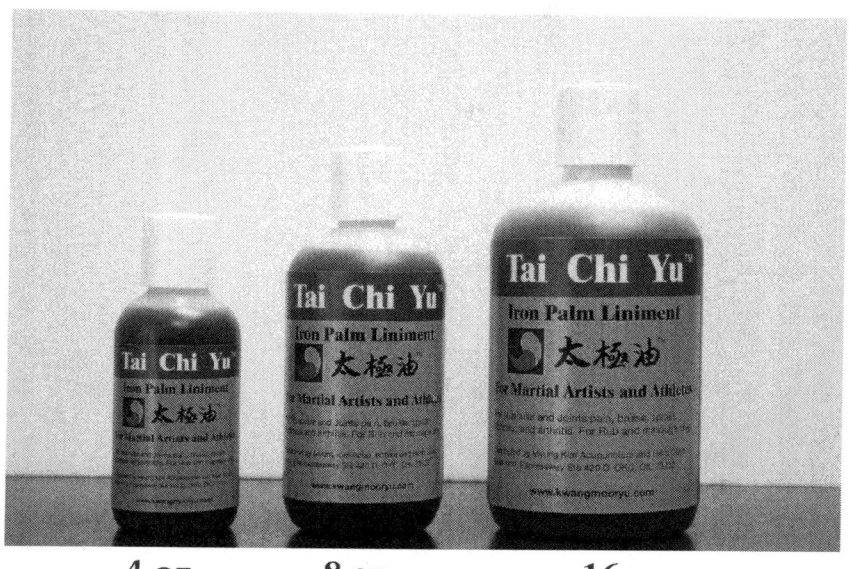

4 oz   8 oz   16 oz

The above photos of **Tai Chi Yu**™ ("iron palm liniment") contains **Dit Da Jow**™ original formula plus very secret family ingredients dissolved in water and glycerin.

Tai Chi Yu™ is great for iron palm training, joint pain, arthritis, ingrown hairs, bruises, psoriasis, itchiness, body odor and minor cuts.

TAI CHI YU ORDER FORM

Please allow 1 to 2 weeks for delivery

[ ] Tai Chi Yu   4 oz Bottle $19.95 ea

[ ] Tai Chi Yu   8 oz Bottle $34.95 ea

[ ] Tai Chi Yu   16 oz Bottle $59.95 ea

ADD $8.95 for S&H per item: + **$8.95**

OKLAHOMA Residents MUST ADD 8.625% TAX

<u>**WE ACCEPT PAYMENT VIA PAYPAL ONLY.**</u>

Email this form invoice and send payment to:

ordersmyungckim@gmail.com

SHIPPING ADDRESS

Name:

Address:

City:

State:

Zip:

Email:

Printed in Great Britain
by Amazon